Library Technology
REPORTS
Expert Guides to Library Systems and Services

RFID in Libraries:
A Step toward Interoperability

Lori Bowen Ayre

ALA TechSource
alatechsource.org

American Library Association

Library Technology
REPORTS

ALA TechSource purchases fund advocacy, awareness, and accreditation programs for library professionals worldwide.

Volume 48, Number 5

RFID in Libraries: A Step toward Interoperability

ISBNs: (print) 978-0-8389-5860-5; (PDF) 978-0-8389-9433-7; (ePub) 978-0-8389-9434-4; (Kindle) 978-0-8389-9436-8.

American Library Association
50 East Huron St.
Chicago, IL 60611-2795 USA
alatechsource.org
800-545-2433, ext. 4299
312-944-6780
312-280-5275 (fax)

Advertising Representative
Patrick Hogan
phogan@ala.org
312-280-3240

Editor
Patrick Hogan
phogan@ala.org
312-280-3240

Copy Editor
Judith Lauber

Production and Design
Tim Clifford, Production Editor
Karen Sheets de Gracia, Manager of Design and Composition

Library Technology Reports (ISSN 0024-2586) is published eight times a year (January, March, April, June, July, September, October, and December) by American Library Association, 50 E. Huron St., Chicago, IL 60611. It is managed by ALA TechSource, a unit of the publishing department of ALA. Periodical postage paid at Chicago, Illinois, and at additional mailing offices. POSTMASTER: Send address changes to Library Technology Reports, 50 E. Huron St., Chicago, IL 60611.

Trademarked names appear in the text of this journal. Rather than identify or insert a trademark symbol at the appearance of each name, the authors and the American Library Association state that the names are used for editorial purposes exclusively, to the ultimate benefit of the owners of the trademarks. There is absolutely no intention of infringement on the rights of the trademark owners.

ALA TechSource
alatechsource.org

Copyright © 2012 Lori Bowen Ayre
All Rights Reserved.

About the Author

Lori Bowen Ayre specializes in automated materials handling (AMH), open source library system software, and RFID. Her company, The Galecia Group (http://galecia.com), serves library clients coast-to-coast from Washington State (King County Library System) to the East Coast (Massachusetts Library System).

Ayre was first published on the topic of RFID in 2005 when she authored "Wireless Tracking in the Library: Benefits, Threats, and Responsibilities" in *RFID-Applications, Security and Privacy* (Addison Wesley). Most recently, Ayre co-authored "Label-Less Library Logistics: Implementing Labor-Saving Practices in Massachusetts' High-Volume Resource Sharing System" which appears in *Collaborative Librarianship*, 2011(3).

Ayer resides in the beautiful Sonoma County (CA) with her partner, Cheryl Gould, where they enjoy a life full of friends, family, numerous beasts, and a lot of talk about libraries.

Abstract

Library Technology Reports (vol. 48, no. 5) "RFID in Libraries: A Step toward Interoperability" by Lori Bowen Ayre explains how RFID works for identification, security, and materials handling. It helps readers evaluate the costs and benefits of implementation. NISO recently approved a new standard for RFID which holds potential for interoperability. This issue of *Library Technology Reports* provides background on the evolution of the standard and discusses issues for libraries and their vendors in migrating to the new standards.

Subscriptions
alatechsource.org/subscribe

Contents

Introduction — 5
   Acknowledgments — 5
   Executive Summary — 6
   Notes — 7

Chapter 1—Library RFID Systems for Identification, Security, and Materials Handling — 9
   RFID Tags — 9
   UHF Tags in Libraries — 10
   RFID Readers — 12
   RFID and AMH — 15
   Notes — 15

Chaper 2—RFID Costs, Benefits, and ROI — 17
   Benefits of Library RFID — 18
   RFID Costs — 18
   Notes — 19

Chapter 3—RFID Standards — 20
   The History of RFID Standards and Policies in the United States — 21
   Components of US Data Profile — 24
   Notes — 26

Chapter 4—Moving Your RFID System to the New US Data Profile — 27
   Considerations for New RFID Implementations — 28
   The RFID Opportunity for Libraries — 30
   Notes — 34

Introduction

It's an interesting time to be writing an issue devoted to RFID. So much has changed for libraries in the last decade. Ten years ago, it seemed like RFID was poised to take off and become a standard piece of library technology. But standards were slow to develop, and e-books were not. While libraries waited for RFID standards to develop, the iPad and Kindle emerged. As a result, libraries are struggling more with DRM, discovery interfaces, and patron authentication systems than with new technologies focused on their physical material.

Today, RFID systems are nothing more than glorified barcodes largely because libraries think that storing only the barcode on the tag is the best way to ensure patron privacy and because the ILS (integrated library system) doesn't support doing much with the tag besides reading the barcode anyway.

To make financial sense, libraries must use RFID more expansively and expansion relies on taking advantage of the new standard. Existing and new systems will have to migrate to the new standard to ensure vendor interoperability and interoperability between libraries. To protect their investment in RFID, libraries need to insist that vendors comply with the new standards to ensure their systems are interoperable with any vendor's hardware.

RFID could be a powerful technology that could change how libraries deal with physical material as well as leverage digital technologies to offer new services. RFID tags will soon be readable by smartphones, but to take advantage, libraries will need to develop new, patron-centric RFID applications.

The fertile ground for RFID adoption is in moving beyond RFID-as-barcode. It may or may not happen. My hope in writing this issue is that libraries will understand how hobbled our use of RFID in libraries is today. If we, as an industry, choose to invest further in this technology, we need to extend the use of RFID beyond circulation and security to resource sharing, materials handling, technical services, and beyond—into wholly new ways that will delight our patrons.

Acknowledgments

Many people have contributed their time and knowledge to me over the past several years as I've focused my attention on RFID. I've benefited from people working with RFID in their libraries who have shared their stories, successes, and struggles. I've benefitted from working with clients evaluating the technology who needed to explore the benefits versus the costs. I've benefitted from the vendors who have shared their deep knowledge of the technology and the industry. Thank you all for helping me paint a realistic portrait of where RFID technology in libraries is today.

I'd like to say a special thank-you to Karen Schneider for helping me clarify my message. Without her insightful feedback, this manuscript would have been full of information but not nearly as useful as a roadmap for libraries critically evaluating RFID.

I'd also like to thank Mick Fortune, who has become a very important colleague even though we've never met. Mick's work with UK libraries on the issue of RFID continues to break new ground, and my work is very much informed by his knowledge and experience.

Thank you also to Terry Jackson, who also provided useful feedback and proofreading to ensure my message made sense to someone just getting started with RFID.

And finally, thank you to my partner, Cheryl Gould, who has had to endure my obsession with RFID for these past several weeks. I think RIFD is an interesting topic, but there are more important things in life than RFID, and being a loving and attentive partner is certainly one of them. Thanks for your patience.

Executive Summary

RFID (radio frequency identification) tags have been used in libraries since 1999, when the National Library of Singapore installed the first system.[1] RFID tags, like barcodes, are used to uniquely identify library material. A barcode tag has the barcode number imprinted on the tag, and the barcode scanner reads that number using optical technology. With RFID, much more information can be stored on the tag, and the tag data is read via radio technology instead of optical technology. Whereas barcode scanners require line of sight to operate, RFID readers just need to be able to detect the tag. This means the reader needs to be within 18 to 20 inches of the tag, but the tag need not be visible (e.g., it can be inside the book).

The last time *Library Technology Reports* dedicated an issue to the topic of RFID, libraries were one of the few markets getting involved with the technology. According to Richard Boss, the author of that 2003 issue, "more than 500,000 RFID systems [were] installed in warehouses and retail establishments worldwide" and fewer than 200 were installed in libraries.[2] Libraries were a small player at that time, but they were one of the few players in the RFID market.

The worldwide RFID marketplace has changed markedly since 2003. RFID tags are used for toll payment and in supply chain systems to identify pallets and containers. They are used to track animals in the wild and patients in hospitals. RFID tags are used to control access, to immobilize vehicles, and to secure nuclear material. A huge market is asset management, where RFID tags are used to keep track of laptops, projectors, and other valuable equipment owned by an organization. RFID technology is used in aerospace, agriculture, apparel, construction, defense, logistics, medical, manufacturing, oil and gas, pharmaceuticals, and more.[3]

Today, RFID spending exceeds $5.85 billion worldwide,[4] and the technology is used in virtually every industry. However, RFID adoption in libraries has not seen this type of explosion. NXP, manufacturer of the integrated circuits that are part of nearly every library RFID tag, reports that some 3,000 libraries worldwide have implemented RFID. So, while libraries were among the first to get involved with RFID, libraries haven't gone very far with it since 2003.

In fact, most of the library RFID components (tags, readers, software) are essentially the same today as they were in 2003. There have been some improvements in the quality of the products offered, but there isn't much difference when it comes to functionality. The vendors providing RFID solutions are also largely the same, although some of the smaller players have disappeared and some have merged.

Between 2003 and today, digital technology has changed the nature of the library collection everywhere. Virtually every library has increased the size of its electronic resources while the size of physical collections has remained flat. RFID is a technology applicable only to physical books, CDs, and DVDs. Many libraries are reluctant to make a big investment in an expensive technology that is potentially only relevant to their physical collections.

Another reason libraries have been reluctant to embrace RFID is the lack of standards. With RFID, standards are a critical issue. The lack of standards has inhibited the adoption of RFID technology.[5] Standards act as a warranty on the library's investment in RFID. Without standards, RFID is a more risky investment. Standards eliminate vendor lock-in and allow for interoperability across different vendors' solutions. With vendor interoperability, libraries can buy their RFID components from any vendor with the expectation that everything will work together.

Standards lead to library and ILS interoperability as well. With library interoperability, libraries can read each other's RFID tags, making resource sharing and interlibrary loan (ILL) transactions more secure and simpler. ILS interoperability will allow libraries to switch from one ILS to another without having to worry that their RFID components will stop working.

To achieve vendor, library, and ILS interoperability, many standards have to fall into place. Some are there, but we still need more.

In the library market, libraries were able to

> "Early RFID implementers are at considerable risk because of the lack of interoperability of proprietary vendor systems. As RFID providers and libraries adopt tags with the data model recommended in this recommended practice, true interoperability that allows libraries to procure the tags, hardware, and software from independent providers and distributors to use with all tags can become a reality. The data model outlined in this document is an essential first step. This model is a key precursor to a world in which a library can procure tags from different vendors, merge collections containing tags from different vendors, and, for the purposes of interlibrary loan, read the tags on items belonging to other libraries."
>
> —NISO RFID Revision Working Group, *RFID in U.S. Libraries, Recommended Practice of the National Information Standards Organization*, NISO RP-6-2012 (Baltimore, MD: NISO, March 2012), v, www.niso.org/apps/group_public/download.php/8269/RP-6-2012_RFID-in_US_Libraries.pdf.

purchase ISO Standard RFID tags as early as 2003. Specifically, ISO 18000-3 made it possible to purchase RFID tags that wouldn't be rendered obsolete by subsequent developments in RFID. But the availability of ISO tags is only one small piece of the standards puzzle.

In an RFID system, tags contain data. In most cases, 1,024 bytes of data can be encoded into memory on the tag. The RFID reader reads the tag, but in order to do so, the reader needs to know what data elements are being used and how the data has been encoded. A data profile is what defines the elements and how they are encoded. In 2011, ISO finalized ISO 28560, which is a standard composed of three parts. Part 1 defines the data elements to be used on the tag, and the other two parts define alternate encoding methods. In March 2012, NISO established the US Data Profile[6] based on ISO 28560-2 (parts 1 and 2). This represents a very large piece of the puzzle. But there's more.

The RFID reader passes the data captured from the tags to another application. In library RFID systems, the reader usually acts as the conduit for getting the information from the tag and sending it to the ILS. Sometimes the information is used by an RFID application (e.g., inventory management module, weeding application), but it very often needs to communicate with the ILS.

SIP2 is the de facto standard for interfacing with the ILS.[7] Thus, an RFID reader is probably using the SIP2 protocol when it reads the information on the tag and passes it to the ILS. Another important protocol for ILS communication is NCIP2. Both SIP2 and NCIP2 primarily address circulation functions. So, when the RFID system is doing circulation tasks (check-in, check-out, renewals), these two protocols provide another important piece of the standardization puzzle.

RFID can be used for weeding, inventorying, ILL, materials handling, and possibly even for providing enhanced content to patrons using RFID-enabled smartphones. But in order to develop these new library RFID applications, we need to be able to interface in more ways with the ILS. In other words, SIP2 and NCIP2 are not sufficient.

SIP3 was recently released by 3M.[8] It provides a bit more functionality, but it is still far from being the solution for handling all the ILS communications libraries need in order to leverage RFID technology. The good news is that Book Industry Communication (BIC), a UK organization sponsored by booksellers, publishers, library professionals, corporations, and the British Library, has developed a framework intended to provide a roadmap for building upon the existing protocols to support development of additional functionality for library RFID systems.

The BIC Library Communications Framework (BLCF) helps identify the areas where new protocols and functionality are needed and provides guidelines for developing those protocols and functions in a way that remains standardized across the library industry.[9] Rather than having each RFID vendor develop its own inventory application (for example), development according to the BLCF will help standardize all RFID inventory applications so that vendor interoperability and ILS interoperability can continue to be assured. So far, this is a UK project, but US libraries would certainly benefit by getting involved.

The BLCF can guide development of additional protocols or serve as a roadmap for expanding upon existing protocols (e.g., SIP4 or NCIP3) so that we can do more with the ILS without veering off into proprietary solutions.

With the US Data Profile finalized, libraries are at a crossroads. Now is the time to push vendors to adhere to the new US Data Profile to ensure vendor and library interoperability. Widespread adoption of the US Data Profile is important for libraries. It is a big step closer to interoperability.

It is also time to think creatively about what else libraries can do with RFID tags. This will require new protocols for communicating with the ILS and development of new functions. Partnering with libraries in the United Kingdom may be the quickest way to make progress in this area.

My hope is that readers of this issue will come to understand how library RFID fits into the larger worldwide RFID and library context and—for libraries opting to use RFID—understand what needs to be done to exploit it so that it functions as the new technology it is and less like the old technology it has thus far replaced.

Notes

1. Connie K. Haley, Kathleen Degnan, and Kathleen Haefliger, "Library RFID Technology Update," December 9, 2008, https://sites.google.com/site/chaley102/Home/library-rfid-technology-update. Some argue that the University of Central Lancashire began a pilot a year earlier.
2. Richard Boss, "RFID Technology for Libraries," *Library Technology Reports* 39, no. 6 (November–December 2003): 16.
3. For information about the range of industries using RFID, see "RFID Business Applications," *RFID Journal* website, www.rfidjournal.com/article/view/1334/1; B. Craig, J. H. Lee, J. Anderson, H. Tsai, Y. Liu, and J. Shuler, "Integration of ARG_US RFID and DOE TRANSCOM, US Department of Energy Decision and Information Services, www.dis.anl.gov/pubs/70368.pdf; and RFIDTags.com, www.rfidtags.com.
4. Raghu Das and Peter Harrop, *RFID Forecasts, Players and Opportunities 2011–2012* (Cambridge, MA: IDTechEx, 2011), www.idtechex.com/research/reports/rfid_forecasts_players_and_opportunities_2011_2021_000250.asp.

5. May Tajima, "The Role of Technology Standardization in RFID Adoption: The Pharmaceutical Context," *International Journal of IT Standards and Standardization Research* 10, no. 1 (January–June 2012): 49.
6. The US Data Profile is available in NISO RFID Revision Working Group, *RFID in U.S. Libraries, Recommended Practice of the National Information Standards Organization*, NISO RP-6-2012 (Baltimore, MD: NISO, March 2012), www.niso.org/apps/group_public/download.php/8269/RP-6-2012_RFID-in_US_Libraries.pdf.
7. The SIP2 protocol is available in "3M Standard Interchange Protocol," version 2.00, document revision 2.10, updated September 17, 1998, http://multimedia.mmm.com/mws/mediawebserver.dyn?dddddd NLXpsdyHedrHeddd4LYP0DDDDC-.
8. See "SIP 3.0 Ready for Implementation," at author's blog, http://galecia.com/blogs/lori-ayre/sip-30-ready-implementation.
9. For more information about the BIC Library Communications Framework (BLCF), see "Library Interoperability Standards: Data Communication Framework for Library Systems," www.bic.org.uk/e4libraries/16/INTEROPERABILITY-STANDARDS.

Chapter 1

Library RFID Systems for Identification, Security, and Materials Handling

Abstract

Chapter 1 of Library Technology Reports *(vol. 48, no. 5) "RFID in Libraries: A Step toward Interoperability" discusses RFID systems being used by libraries today, which include tags, readers, and software. Libraries place tags in books and other library material to speed materials handling functions such as check-in and check-out and to provide security for the items. This chapter introduces the technology and explains how it is currently used in libraries.*

Library RFID systems are composed of tags, readers, and middleware software. The systems rely heavily on the integrated library system (ILS), and the middleware is designed to support communication between the reader and the ILS. Tags are placed inside library material, on media cases, or on multipart set bags. The readers are placed at staff workstations and self-check machines and built into security gates. At this time, most tags contain only the barcode number of the item and, in some cases, some additional information that can be used by the security system. The readers read the information on the tag (e.g., the barcode) and pass the information to the ILS.

RFID Tags

RFID tags come in many sizes and shapes and varying degrees of rigidity and flexibility depending on how they'll be used. They can be embedded in cardboard, plastic, wood, textiles, and even human or animal tissue. RFID tags can be found in thermal transfer labels, plastic cards, key fobs, and passports. When embedding the tags in a material, it is important to ensure that the components of the surrounding material protect the chip and antenna without creating interference during communications. Therefore, tags are manufactured for specific purposes.

Tags can be passive or active. Passive systems rely on the reader to generate the energy that will allow the tag to transmit the data on the chip. Active tags have their own transmitter and a power source (possibly a battery), so they can transmit the information stored on the chip without relying on the reader's power. RFID tags can be low frequency (LF), high frequency (HF), or ultra high frequency (UHF); see table 1.1. NFC (near field communication) is a kind of HF RFID tag.

The tags used in library applications are HF tags. They look like thin paper labels (see figure 1.1). In fact, some libraries imprint their library logo on the tags so they function as property labels as well.

Library book tags are designed to be placed into books. The antenna is tuned so that when the tag is placed inside the book, the book's material (book cover and paper) won't degrade, or detune, the signal. Items designed for CDs and DVDs are also specially tuned to work with the hard plastic that makes up a DVD or CD. Book tags wouldn't work well if used on a CD or DVD, and media tags wouldn't work well on a book because of the detuning effect of the material to which they are affixed.

Most libraries use HF tags for library applications because the read range is shorter and because the standards have thus far specified HF tags. However, the RFID marketplace is changing rapidly, driven largely by the popularity of UHF applications.

RFID Tags	Low Frequency (LF)	High Frequency (HF)	Ultra High Frequency (UHF)
Frequency	125 kHz	13.56 MHz	400 MHz to 1 GHz
Operating Distance	30 cm to 1 m	10 cm to 1 m	Passive: up to 25 m Active: up to 100 m
Characteristics	Short read range. Read range is easier to control. Handle metal and water better than UHF. Can be affected by industrial noise. Slower data transfer rate. Cannot always communicate with multiple tags.	Short read range (especially NFC tags). Read range easier to control than UHF. Not as effective as LF in presence of metal and water, but better than UHF. Unaffected by industrial noise. Can communicate with multiple tags simultaneously.	Long read range. Fast reading of multiple tags. Less tag memory than HF. Poor performance around liquids and metals. Operate in a crowded frequency.
Applications		Library materials management and security, access control, banking cards, contactless payment systems, goods control, security.	Asset tracking, supply chain, logistics, toll booths, real-time locating systems, container security, library material management and security (limited).

Table 1.1
Types of RFID tags

Figure 1.1
48 mm x 80 mm TAGSYS Folio 370-F3 tag. Photo provided courtesy of TAGSYS. See "Folio HF RFID Tags," datasheet, TAGSYS RFID website, 2012, http://tagsysrfid.com/content/download/463/3044/version/3/file/T-M-FolioTags-Datasheet-6Mar2012.pdf.

Book Tags

HF book tags come in two shapes. One is credit card size (figure 1.2) and one is square (figure 1.3). Both use NXP microchips, most often with 1,024 bytes of memory, and operate at 13.56 MHz. The different shapes are the result of the antenna design. The main manufacturers of library RFID tags are TAGSYS and SMARTRAC.[1] But libraries don't buy directly from the manufacturer. Libraries buy the tags from a library RFID vendor.[2]

Media Tags

The tags used for CDs and DVDs (figure 1.4) also come in two form factors: disk hub tags and full coverage tags. Hub tags fit on the inside ring of the CD or DVD and have not proven to be nearly as effective as the full coverage tags. The full coverage tags cover one side of the CD or DVD. The antenna is much bigger on these tags because it runs around the outside edge of the CD or DVD instead of the inside ring.

Two manufacturers make the full coverage tags: UPM Raflatac was the original manufacturer of the popular Stingray tag. Now that SMARTRAC owns UPM, the Stingray tag is simply known as the CDlabel.[3]

The other company making the full coverage tags was FCI Smartag, which manufactured the X-Range. This company has now been purchased by the Identive Group.[4]

UHF Tags in Libraries

When libraries first began using RFID, the only viable tag for item-level tracking was an HF tag. This is

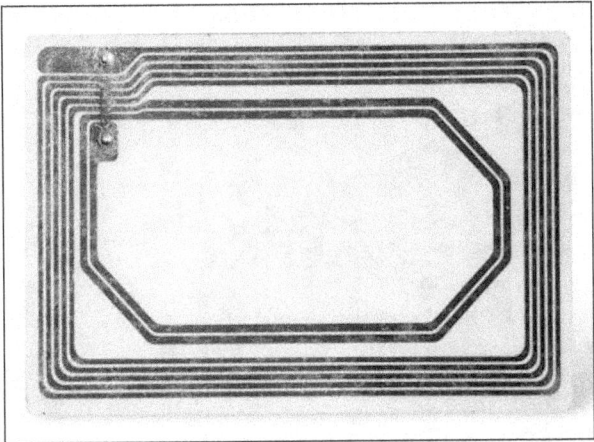

Figure 1.2
3M's ISO RFID tag. Photo courtesy of 3M. See "ISO RFID Tags," 3M website, http://solutions.3m.com/wps/portal/3M/en_US/3MLibrarySystems/Home/Products/RFIDTags.

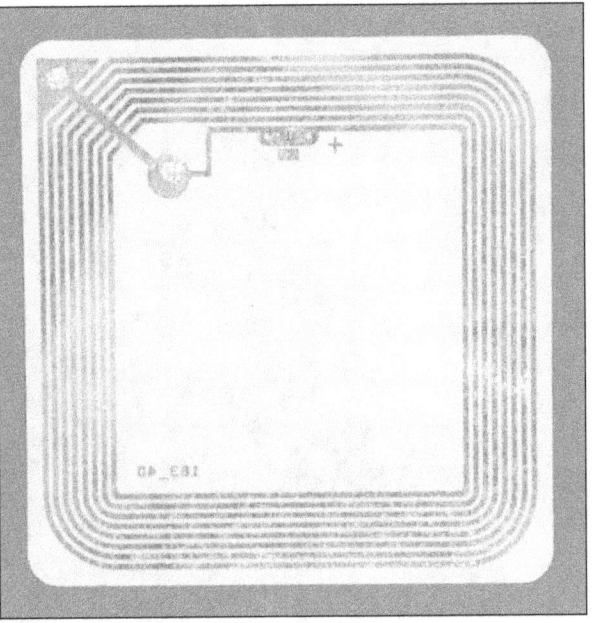

Figure 1.3
RFID Library Solution's square book tag. Image courtesy of RFID Library Solutions. See "RFID Products," RFID Library Solutions website, www.rfidlibrarysolutions.com/#!rfid-products.

because the read range of UHF is longer and more unwieldy than HF tags, and because early UHF tags encountered problems around metal and water. However, UHF technology has evolved quite a bit, and many RFID experts assert it is equally effective for item-level tracking. Some argue that it is a better choice than HF because UHF tags are more universal.[5]

However, virtually all US library RFID systems in production are based on HF tags.[6] There may soon be one exception. At the end of this year, Grand Rapids Public Library expects to go live with its UHF system. Grand Rapids has developed an open source solution for its UHF RFID system for communicating with its ILS (which is Evergreen, also an open source product). It is currently pilot testing and plans to go live with the new system in July 2012.

UHF technology has evolved very fast in the last several years and is now widely adopted for item-level tracking. Between 2003 and now, as other industries were focusing on UHF tags and developing standards and new applications across numerous industries, libraries continued to focus their standards efforts only on HF tags.

In 2006, EPC Gen 2 became the standard for item-level tagging with UHF tags. However, most library efforts to develop a data model and encoding standard have focused on the ISO 18000-3, Mode 1 standard for HF tags instead of the EPC Gen 2 standard for UHF. The exception is in Asia and to some degree in Australia. There are two proposals in the works that address the technical specifications of UHF tags for library use. At least one of them provides an approach that would help with interoperability across UHF systems (not between UHF and HF systems) and would leverage the data elements specified by ISO 28560-1 (for use with HF systems).

Figure 1.4
A full coverage media tag (StingRay) ready to be applied.

Given the pervasiveness of UHF tags for item-level tracking in so many other industries, it isn't entirely clear that the decision to standardize on HF tags in libraries was the right choice. How to explore UHF tags for libraries without disrupting the progress made toward standardization and interoperability remains a conundrum for everyone involved in standards development. It is a question that should be resolved as

Figure 1.5
Example of an RFID reader that can be placed on top of the counter or underneath. Photo courtesy of Bibliotheca. See "Smartgate 100/200/300," Bibliotheca website, www.bibliotheca.com/1/index.php/gallery?productCode=s_station100.200.300 &productTitle=smartgate%20100/200/300.

soon as possible so that libraries can move forward in unison and not at cross-purposes.

RFID Readers

Implementing RFID generally requires installing an RFID reader in every place where a barcode scanner is installed. This means that all staff workstations, self-check machines, and security gates must be configured with an RFID reader or replaced.

RFID-Enabled Staff Stations

RFID readers for staff stations are flat pads which can be placed on or under counters (figure 1.5). Once the material gets close enough to the reader, the tags are read and the data conveyed to the ILS. A stack of books can be placed in the pad's read range and as the tags are read, data is passed to the ILS.

The RFID readers used at staff workstations require that software be installed at the workstation to assist with the communication between the reader and the ILS. Sometimes the software is a "keyboard wedge," meaning it simply translates the data read by the device into keyboard data. Other times, the software is more sophisticated and enhances the circulation process. Some library RFID solutions work well with one ILS and less well with another. Therefore, before settling on an RFID solution, it is very important to test the software integration at staff workstations with your specific ILS.

Self-Check Machines

According to the 2012 Library RFID Survey[7] (an international survey in which 470 people from 278 libraries responded), 98 percent of libraries that have implemented RFID are using it for self-service.[8] This is because RFID-based self-check is easier for patrons to use because the patron doesn't have to identify the barcode and align the item properly. Patrons can just

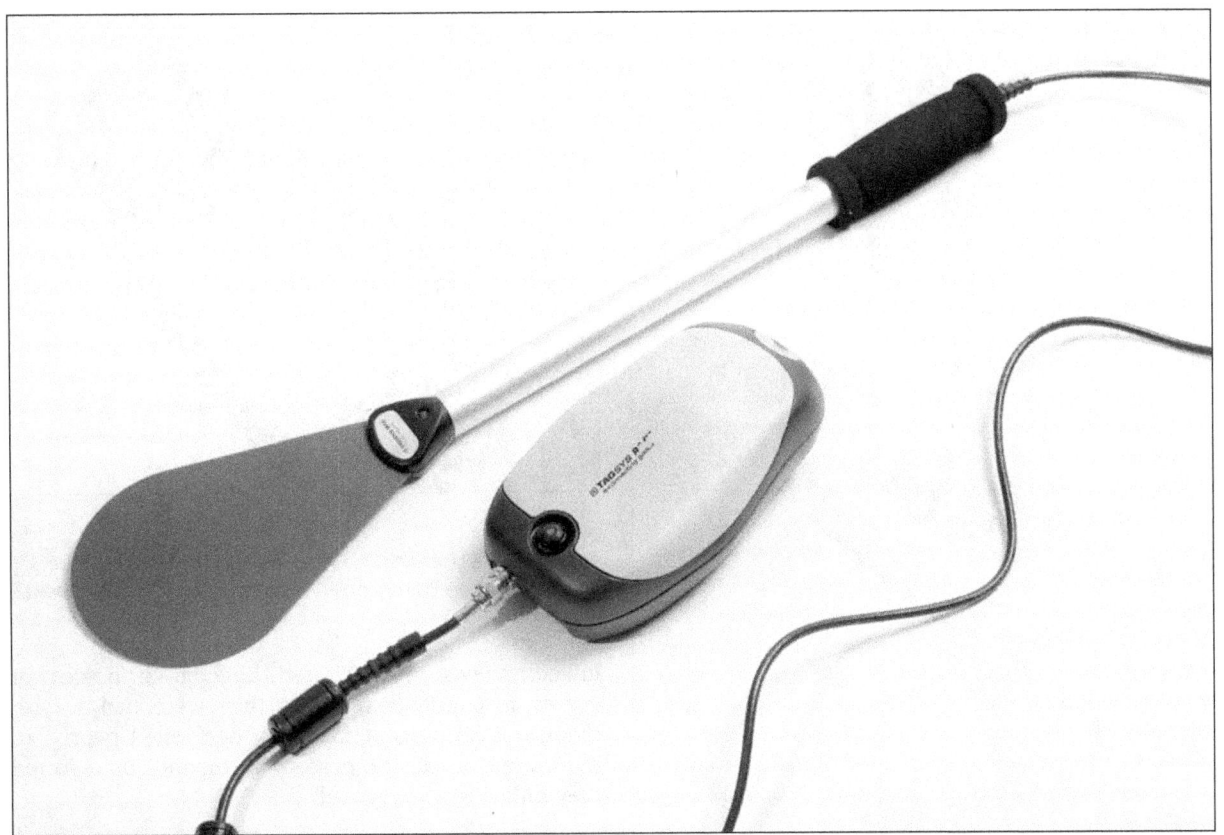

Figure 1.6
Portable inventory system from Tech-Logic. Photo courtesy of Tech-Logic.
See "CircTRAK," Tech Logic website, www.tech-logic.com/solutions/rfid/inventory-control.asp.

set their books on the counter and the system begins reading them, making check-out very easy.

However, for RFID-based self-check to be widely adopted, patrons have to be able to do all of their check-outs at the self-check machine. If CDs or DVDs require staff intervention to open the case or get the media, or if some category of library material isn't RFID tagged, the percentage of self-service check-outs will be low. According to the 2012 survey, only 35 percent of respondents reported 85 percent or higher self-check use even though their systems were RFID based.[9]

Most self-check machines can be easily upgraded to support RFID.

Security Gates

Security gates are the second most implemented RFID product in libraries, after self-check machines. According to the 2012 survey, 85 percent of libraries that have implemented RFID are using them for security.[10]

Security gates used in libraries have traditionally used EM (electromagnetic) systems to detect items that have not been checked out. With an EM-based system, the item must be sensitized (security turned on) or desensitized (security turned off) as items are checked in and checked out. To turn on the EM system in a book or CD, the item is dragged past a magnet that sensitizes or desensitizes the strip. These sensitizers are bulky pieces of equipment that add a step in the circulation workflow (for both patrons and staff) and take up a lot of space on the countertop—or worse, require a staff person to do the sensitizing at a separate workstation equipped with such a unit.

RFID tags can be used for identification and circulation as well as security. Security is handled by changing one piece of information on the RFID's microchip as the item is checked in and out. It does not require an additional piece of equipment or additional work for the patron and staff.

The effectiveness of RFID versus EM security is roughly equal. Neither is perfect. Although several tags can be read at once, various conditions can result in items going undetected through the RFID security gates. If a person passes through the gates with a large number of picture books, it is more difficult to detect all the tags because the tags may be overlapping. When tags are close together and overlap, they can interfere with one another. Sometimes items can be missed if they are held in just the right position (e.g., the exact center of the gates where they may be just out of range

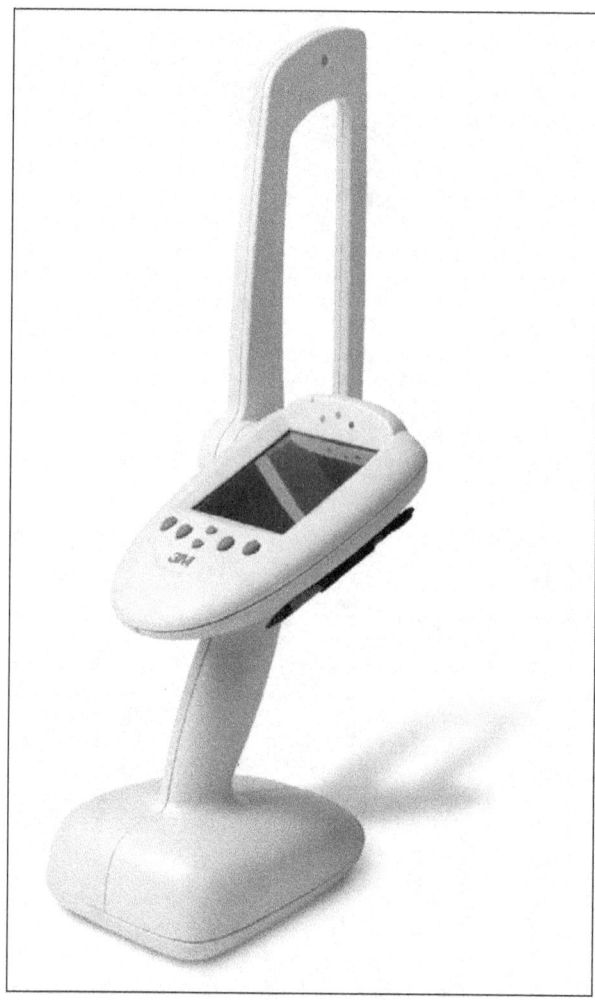

Figure 1.7
3M Digital Library Assistant. Photo courtesy of 3M. See "Digital Library Assistant," 3M website, http://solutions.3m.com/wps/portal/3M/en_US/3MLibrarySystems/Home/Products/RFIDCollectionManagement.

of both readers). Also, CDs and DVDs pose challenges for RFID systems because of the metal in some DVDs and because they too can overlap.

Despite these challenges, RFID security is as effective as EM security systems have been. They act as a theft deterrent, not as theft prevention. And unlike EM strips, they don't require additional processing (adding the EM strip) and handling (sensitizing and desensitizing).

RFID security should be used if a library is implementing an RFID system; however, better security shouldn't be the library's primary justification for switching from a barcode/EM system to RFID.

Converting from EM to RFID can be expensive as it may require replacing all the library's existing security gates. Recently, at least one vendor has made a hybrid security gate available. It's not clear how effective they are, however. According to the 2012 Library RFID Survey, the hybrid security gates are getting

Figure 1.8
EnvisionWare LibraryPDA. Photo courtesy of EnvisionWare. See "LibraryPDA," EnvisionWare website, http://envisionware.com/librarypda.

mixed reviews. In the United Kingdom, 50 percent of survey respondents reported they were happy with them, but 38 percent said they performed poorly. In the United States, 100 percent of respondents reported they didn't work very well.[11]

Mobile Readers

There are two form factors in library mobile readers: wands and handhelds (figures 1.6–1.8). Some of the mobile readers used for inventory are configured with long handles or wands in order to better read the tags on material shelved high and low. Other mobile readers are attached to handheld computers so the devices can be used for weeding, finding lost material, identifying items on the pull list, and shelf reading. These units often allow the staff person to download information to the device (e.g., weed list or lost items list) and have the ability to upload the updated information back to the ILS.

RFID Software

Every manufacturer of library RFID systems provides its own proprietary software to run its RFID equipment. In general, this goes beyond simply a "hardware driver" that allows the equipment to work with an operating system.

Sophisticated RFID software takes advantage of the fact that the data from several tags can be captured at once (unlike the "keyboard wedge" mentioned earlier). Rather than feeding the data to the ILS one keystroke at a time, numerous "calls" can be made to the ILS to get work done. These calls are usually SIP2 calls, meaning the RFID application communicates with the SIP2 server, which in turn communicates with the

ILS. Communicating with the SIP2 server is how all self-service check-out transactions are handled whether via barcode or RFID. The difference is in the middleware's ability to read all the tags at once, sort out the information needed to be sent, and sending only that information. The rest of the transaction is handled by the ILS and the self-check machine and has nothing to do with RFID specifically.

But not all transactions can be handled by the library's SIP2 server. Some things that can be done with RFID hardware are not supported by SIP2. In this case, it is up to the RFID application to do the work. This applies to tasks such as weeding, inventory, and generating pull lists, and it could apply to many more functions as yet undefined. In these cases, the RFID vendor has written proprietary software that is the vendor's intellectual property. New protocols need to be developed so that RFID vendors can use standardized methods for accessing the ILS and sending data to the ILS beyond the basic circulation functions that are now supported by SIP2 and NCIP2.

RFID and AMH

Many people are under the mistaken impression that a library cannot implement automated check-in or sorting without RFID. In fact, automated materials handling (AMH) systems can function very well in either environment.

One-at-a-Time Check-in Systems

AMH systems that rely on a person feeding in items one at a time can use barcodes or RFID tags. The only difference is that the person inducting material into a barcode-based system must orient the material properly. If the item is placed with the barcode facing down or if the barcode is inside the book, the scanner won't be able to read it. AMH systems can be designed to open book covers or can be equipped with scanners above and below the items so the barcode *can* be read even if a patron inserts a book upside-down. Obviously, the system will cost a bit more if two scanners are needed at the induction points.

The advantage of one-at-a-time check-in systems (whether barcode- or RFID-based) is that each return is verified and the customer can get a receipt.

Book Drop Style Check-in Systems

Some AMH systems behave more like traditional book drops, allowing the patron to dump the books into

> *RFID security should be used if a library is implementing an RFID system; however, better security shouldn't be the library's primary justification for switching from a barcode/EM system to RFID.*

a receptacle rather than feeding them in one a time. These systems can also be used with either barcodes or RFID tags.

Whether the items have barcodes or RFID tags, each item must be checked in one at a time eventually. To do this requires that the system move items up a slanted conveyor section at least two feet long. The conveyor is angled such that the library material slides apart and each item ends up separated (singulated) by the time it reaches the scanner or RFID reader.[12] If the system is barcode-based, it will be necessary to have scanners above and below the items to ensure the barcode can be scanned.

The key advantage to these drop-in types of systems is they are easier for patrons to use when they have a lot of material to return. There are two disadvantages to these systems. One is that patrons can't get a receipt for their returns because the items aren't checked in right away. The other is that this type of sorter takes up more room. Both of these disadvantages are a result of how the items are singulated after being dropped in.

The one type of book return that can be used with RFID, but not barcodes, is the RFID-enabled book drop (without the sorter). The book drop is simply configured with an RFID reader so that items get checked in as they are dropped in. The only advantage of these systems is for the customer who assumes all of the items have been successfully checked in. For staff, there is no advantage because each item will need to be checked in again to determine how it should be handled.

Notes

1. SMARTRAC bought two other big players in the market, UPM and KSW. For more information, see "SMARTRAC Further Strengthens Its Trusted Brand," news release, SMARTRAC website, March 1, 2012, www.smartrac-group.com/en/media-relations-latest-press-releases.php?type=pm_home&id=344&year=2012, and "SMARTRAC Completes UPM RFID Transaction," FreshNews.com, April 1, 2012, www.freshnews.com/news/631216/smartrac-completes-upm-rfid-transaction.
2. For a listing of vendors providing RFID products and services related to RFID, see "Buyers Guide," *American Libraries* website, http://americanlibrariesbuyersguide.com/.
3. See "CDlabel," datasheet, SMARTRAC Technologies,

2009, www.smartrac-group.com/en/download_2/datasheets/SMARTRAC_Datasheet_CD_Label.pdf.
4. See "Identive Group Announces Closing of Smartag Acquisition," news release, Identive website, November 22, 2010, www.identive-group.com/en/index.php?option=com_k2&view=item&id=156:identive-group-announces-closing-of-smartag-acquisition&Itemid=246.
5. J. Uddin, M. B. I. Reaz, M. A. Hassan, A. N. Nordin, M. I. Ibrahimy, and M. A. M. Ali, "UHF RFID Antenna Architectures and Applications," full length research paper, *Science Research and Essays* 5, no. 10 (May 18, 2010): 1034, www.academicjournals.org/sre/pdf/pdf2010/18May/Uddin%20et%20al.pdf.
6. Carver County (MN) has an RFID system, but it is not in production. It is doing tests in partnership with 3M. See NISO RFID Revision Working Group, *RFID in U.S. Libraries,* Recommended Practice of the National Information Standards Organization, NISO RP-6-2012 (Baltimore, MD: NISO, March 2012), 50, www.niso.org/apps/group_public/download.php/8269/RP-6-2012_RFID-in_US_Libraries.pdf.
7. Mick Fortune has been conducting surveys about library RFID use in the United Kingdom since 2009. In 2011, Alan Butters and I worked with him to make the survey applicable to our markets (Australia and North America), and we encouraged libraries in those two markets to respond. Fifty-one US libraries responded, compared to 115 from the United Kingdom and 58 from Australia plus several from 13 other countries. All of the survey responses can be found at Mick Fortune, "Search Results for: 2012 library rfid survey," *RFID—Changing Libraries for Good?* (blog), www.mickfortune.com/Wordpress/?s=2012+library+rfid+survey.
8. Mick Fortune, "Using RFID in the Library—Part 3 of the 2012 Survey," *RFID—Changing Libraries for Good?* (blog), March 6, 2012, www.mickfortune.com/Wordpress/?p=747#more-747.
9. Mick Fortune, "2012 Library RFID Survey: Self Service," www.libraryrfid.co.uk/useselfservice.html.
10. Mick Fortune, "2012 Library RFID Survey—Part 4," *RFID—Changing Libraries for Good?* (blog), March 8, 2012, www.mickfortune.com/Wordpress/?p=757.
11. Mick Fortune, "2012 Library RFID Survey—Part 6," *RFID—Changing Libraries for Good?* (blog), March 19, 2012, www.mickfortune.com/Wordpress/?p=775.
12. See the video "UltraSort Patented Item Deshingler" at "UltraSort Systems," Tech Logic website, www.tech-logic.com/solutions/ast/ultrasort.asp.

Chapter 2

RFID Costs, Benefits, and ROI

Abstract

Chapter 2 of Library Technology Reports *(vol. 48, no. 5) "RFID in Libraries: A Step toward Interoperability" discusses the costs and benefits associated with RFID, which can be a fairly expensive technology. RFID requires purchasing tags and placing them in every item in the library's collection. In addition, many hardware components need to be upgraded to work with RFID systems. However, there are also several benefits. This chapter spells out the specific costs and benefits and provides guidance for how to evaluate the return on investment.*

The return on investment for a library RFID system has thus far not been clearly established.[1] While some have argued that a library RFID system will pay for itself within two to three years because of the reductions in staff time,[2] this is likely true in very few library environments. Libraries facing significant reductions in staff have found they were able to handle many more circulation transactions per person with RFID than without. In many cases, the RFID implementation is also tied to a transition to more self-service, so it is often difficult to tie the savings specifically to RFID.

Jeff Narver of 3M suggests that libraries can expect a three- to seven-year investment payback ("dependent on some variables"),[3] and this is more consistent with my experience as a library RFID consultant. Determining payback period for RFID is more art than science because each library's situation is different (whether it had self-check systems before RFID was implemented or not, how much circulation it does and how that's changed, staffing levels before and after, etc.). In general, it is safe to say that fewer staff members can circulate the same amount of material with RFID or the same number of staff members can circulate more material.[4] However, being able to circulate more material with fewer staff members doesn't make a cogent return on investment argument, especially given the industry-wide transition to more and more digital content and fewer physical items.

The argument in favor of RFID for academic libraries is even more difficult because circulation is not a high-volume business. In fact, the academic library's traditional role "as a repository of physical books and periodicals is quickly fading."[5] Determining the return on investment will involve evaluating resource sharing, security, and perhaps new RFID applications to determine if the benefits justify the costs.

One of the reasons the ROI argument is challenging is because libraries are using RFID tags as barcodes on steroids.[6] And while RFID certainly "lubes" all self-service and materials handling workflows and provides security on the items at the same time, the improvements are relatively modest given the costs.

Based on how high-circulating libraries use RFID today, they are often much better off purchasing an AMH system (automated check-in system with three or more sorts) if their objective is to reduce operating expenses (e.g., reduce staff costs). RFID implementations typically cost hundreds of thousands of dollars by the time you buy the tags, do the tagging, and upgrade or replace all the security gates, staff workstations, and self-check machines. A small AMH system can be had for under $50,000. An automated check-in system moves the entire check-in workflow from staff to patron, and there's no better way to reduce the circulation staff workload than self-service.

However, RFID makes the workflow less labor-intensive not just for staff, but for patrons as well. So if improving the customer's experience and reducing repetitive staff tasks are high priorities, RFID may make sense for you. In addition, libraries looking to implement a security solution are often better off choosing RFID than implementing an EM solution, which only gets you the security function without the other benefits of RFID.

As it stands today, RFID continues to be a very expensive solution to "too much circulation" and "too few staff." The compelling argument for RFID will come when vendor components are interoperable and new RFID applications are developed that completely change staff and materials handling workflows and result in new services for patrons.

Benefits of Library RFID

The NISO RFID Revision Working Group suggests that the benefits of adopting RFID technology may include the following:

a. Reduction of staff manual processes, errors, and repetitive motion
b. Enhanced customer experience through fast and private self check-outs
c. Reduction of staff and patron time spent on finding items
d. Integrated security functionality[7]

Reduction in Staff Manual Processes, Errors, and Repetitive Motion

The most significant tangible benefit of installing RFID is reducing the need to grasp, pick up, and manipulate items during the check-in and check-out process. In addition to speeding up the process (by allowing staff to check out several items at a time, rather than having to scan each item individually), RFID reduces the potential for repetitive stress injuries because of the reduction in "grasping" motions. Staff don't have to handle a barcode scanner or position the material in any particular way for the item to be read. Five or six items can be read at once simply by stacking them on the counter.

Enhanced Customer Experience through Fast and Private Self Check-outs

RFID-tagged material improves the self check-out process for customers. Not only are the tags more easily read by the self check-out machines, but multiple items can be read at once, making self check-out even faster and easier. Patrons can more easily check out material without having to distinguish barcodes from ISBNs and without having to open the covers when barcodes have been placed inside the books.

Another benefit of RFID self check-out is that it is completely private. Patrons can check out items without having to present them to library staff.

Reduction in Staff and Patron Time Spent on Finding Items

Both staff and patrons are frustrated when they go to the shelf to find an item listed as "on shelf" and it is nowhere to be found. However, few libraries inventory their entire collection regularly because it is so labor-intensive. But when libraries discontinue inventorying their collections, it is almost impossible to know how much material is lost due to theft and to ensure that material that is placed on hold is actually available and on the shelf.

Using the RFID mobile readers, regular inventories become manageable. By using handheld readers, inventorying and finding items to pull for holds, weeding, and shelf reading can be done in a fraction of the time previously needed. All the items on a shelf can be identified by passing a portable reader past each item without needing to handle them and also without requiring staff to read the labels on the spine. The portable readers can identify items that are misshelved or missing or that need to be pulled to fill a hold.

Integrated Security Functionality

RFID tags can be used for material identification as well as material security. Libraries no longer need an EM security strip for security. Instead of the additional step of sensitizing or desensitizing materials at check-in and check-out, security is enabled or disabled automatically as part of the check-in and check-out process. No additional handling and no EM equipment is necessary. Security is enabled or disabled as the items are stacked upon or slid over an RFID-enabled pad at each workstation.

Libraries report other reasons for choosing RFID. According to the 2012 Library RFID Survey, one of the most important reasons US libraries adopted RFID technology was to save costs. Of US respondents, 68 percent said this was a very important reason.[8] Based on some of the comments included in the survey, very often the incentive was to extend hours or handle more work with less staff. In other words, the cost savings were in staff that were not hired to handle the increased workload.

RFID Costs

Tag Costs

As of this writing, the cost of basic book tags has fallen to under 20 cents each. The full-coverage tags used on media are closer to 65 cents, but because of all the consolidations in the marketplace, these prices may go even lower. However, the price of HF library tags will probably never reach the five-cent mark that many people had hoped to see. This expectation was based on the costs of UHF tags which are cheaper and used much more widely around the world. These tags are used in supply chain applications where they are essentially disposable. Billions of UHF tags are sold annually. This is, of course, not the case for library RFID tags. Many fewer library tags are sold, and the tags must endure numerous circulations (several read/write transactions) and a lot of handling by people using the books, as well as people (and machines) sorting the books. They must be designed to handle the hard work of being a circulating library item.

Tagging Costs

Applying RFID tags to every item in the collection can be done with in-house staff, or it can be outsourced. The benefit of outsourcing is that the work can generally be done more quickly. The benefit of doing it in-house is that it is generally cheaper.

Libraries that do their own tagging report tagging speeds of 350 to 400 items per hour.[9] The most efficient way to do the tagging is to have a two-person team use a mobile cart with a laptop and RFID reader, a roll of tags, and a barcode scanner. Many RFID vendors sell or lease mobile carts that can be used for RFID conversions. Programming the tags involves scanning the barcode to encode the barcode number on the tag and then placing the tag inside the book. Many libraries mark the book so they know which ones have been tagged before reshelving them.

Tagging can also be outsourced[10] for a set amount per tag applied (around 30 cents each).

Equipment Costs

One of the biggest costs associated with implementing RFID is the cost of purchasing or upgrading equipment to work with the RFID tags. For example, every workstation that now has a barcode scanner will need an RFID reader, and often the security gates will need to be replaced with RFID-based security gates. Security gates can cost upwards of $10,000, so depending on the number of exits that require new gates, the cost of replacing them can increase the cost of the RFID conversion project dramatically.

Automated check-in systems, sorters, and self check-out machines will also need to be converted to support RFID. In some cases, the units have to be replaced, but in many cases, the self-check vendor can modify existing barcode-based units to work with RFID tags as well. Expect to spend $2,000 to $5,000 per self-service check-in and check-out, plus each sorter induction that needs to be upgraded from barcode to RFID.

To perform inventory, most vendors offer some kind of portable device. These devices are optional insofar as they are not required to perform basic check-in and check-out functions. However, one of the primary benefits is the relative ease with which inventory can be performed with one. Ideally, each library outlet should have its own portable RFID reader to use for weeding, shelf reading, pulling items to fill holds, and performing inventory. These units can cost between $5,000 and $10,000 each.

Notes

1. Karen Coyle and Elena Engel studied California RFID implementations and developed a protocol for establishing ROI but recommended doing so with ten years' worth of data, which was unavailable at that time (2006). More information available at Karen Coyle, "California State Library Study on RFID and Return on Investment," Karen Coyle's Home Page, http://kcoyle.net/rfid_roi.html.
2. Connie K. Haley, Kathleen Degnan, and Kathleen Haefliger, "Library RFID Technology Update," December 9, 2008, https://sites.google.com/site/chaley102/Home/library-rfid-technology-update.
3. Jeff Narver, "Top 10 Reasons Why Canadian Public Libraries Implement RFID," 3M website, February 2007, http://multimedia.3m.com/mws/mediawebserver?mwsId=SSSSSu7zK1fslxtUN8t1NY_eev7qe17zHvTSevTSeSSSSSS--&fn=WhyPublicLibrariesImplRFID.pdf.
4. Elena Engel, "RFID Implementations in California Libraries: Costs and Benefits," July 2006, Karen Coyle's Home Page, http://kcoyle.net/RFIDCostsBenefits.pdf.
5. University Leadership Council, *Redefining the Academic Library: Managing the Migration to Digital Information Services* (Washington, DC: University Leadership Council, 2011), viii, www.educationadvisoryboard.com/pdf/23634-EAB-Redefining-the-Academic-Library.pdf.
6. "Juiced" barcodes in the current vernacular.
7. NISO RFID Revision Working Group, *RFID in U.S. Libraries,* Recommended Practice of the National Information Standards Organization, NISO RP-6-2012 (Baltimore, MD: NISO, March 2012), 1, www.niso.org/apps/group_public/download.php/8269/RP-6-2012_RFID-in_US_Libraries.pdf.
8. Mick Fortune, "Why Do Libraries Invest in RFID?—Part Two of This Year's Survey," *RFID—Changing Libraries for Good?* (blog), March 5, 2012, www.mickfortune.com/Wordpress/?p=739.
9. The US Data Profile document (see note 7 above) reports tagging speeds "approaching 500 items per hour with two-person teams." A 3M study found customers using their conversion stations tagged 400 items per hour (per team). See "3M RFID Systems Deliver ROI for Libraries," www.3m.com/library.
10. The companies providing tagging services at this time include Backstage Library Works (www.bslw.com), RFID Library Solutions (http://rfidlibrarysolutions.com), and AMH & RFID Consultants (http://amhrfid.com).

Chapter 3

RFID Standards

Abstract

Chapter 3 of Library Technology Reports *(vol. 48, no. 5) "RFID in Libraries: A Step toward Interoperability" discusses RFID standards. RFID has not been widely adopted in libraries partly because of the lack of standards. However, as of 2012, several key standards are in place, which provides an opportunity for moving toward interoperable RFID systems where libraries should be able to read each other's RFID tags, and tags and equipment should all work together regardless of the vendor or the library system being used. This chapter provides a brief history of the standards development process and articulates what needs to be done to take advantage of the standards now in place.*

One of the reasons RFID has not been more widely adopted in libraries is the lack of standards. Without standards, libraries couldn't be assured that their significant investment would be worthwhile. Those libraries that did go ahead and take the plunge early on have had to deal with the fallout of being early adopters: the need to replace tags, replace hardware, and find new vendors to support their proprietary systems. Libraries that had to replace their tags were in the toughest position because RFID tags cannot be simply pulled off a book or DVD. In fact, they cannot be removed from a CD or DVD, in most cases, without destroying the media. At least with books, it may be possible to disable the tag (sometimes by cutting the antenna) and then put another RFID tag inside the book (being careful to place it where it won't interfere with the old tag). Replacing RFID tags is not something you want to do if you can somehow avoid it.

Standards provide insurance that a library's investment in technology will benefit it in both the short term and long term. Standards also help ensure that old practices don't restrict the ways that new technology is employed. While it is easy for libraries to use RFID tags as glorified barcodes (writing only the barcode number on the tag), it is an unnecessarily limited way to use the technology. Standards provide guidelines for extending the use of RFID tags for libraries as well as the other stakeholders who could also benefit from reading or writing data to the tags.

Standards that take the entire life cycle of a library item into account can help ensure that the RFID tags are usable at each stage (e.g., supplier, jobber, retail, library, used bookstore). Suppliers, distributors, and retailers of books can benefit from RFID tags in books as much as libraries can. However, how the supplier or retailer uses the tags will be very different from how a library uses the tags. For example, there may be fields that the retailers find very useful (e.g., Title) that a library would choose to leave blank to ensure patron privacy is protected.

Data model standards specify fields that should be left "unlocked" to give maximum flexibility to everyone in the supply chain. Once an item moves from manufacturer to jobber to library, the library should have the option to limit the data written to the tag as it sees fit, keeping in mind its commitment to protecting patron privacy. Similarly, the way a library uses the tag should not impede how others in the book industry choose to use the tag.

Libraries also benefit from having tags placed in books well in advance of arriving in the library. While moving through the supply chain, these tagged books can be more efficiently managed, thereby reducing everyone's costs. Also, upstream suppliers could provide information on the tag that supports the library's receiving workflows (e.g., Supplier ID and Order Number).

The History of RFID Standards and Policies in the United States

It has been a long road to a comprehensive US Data Profile that specifies the tag that should be used in library implementations (ISO 18000-3, Mode 1) and what elements should be used and how they should be encoded (ISO 28560-2). It is worth a quick review of some of the issues that have been raised along the way and how they have been addressed in the revised recommendations from NISO (aka US Data Profile).[1]

Book Industry Study Group RFID Policy Statement (2004)

In 2004, the Book Industry Study Group convened an RFID task force of organizations related to the creation, publishing, distribution, and retail sales of books and their use in libraries. The goal of the task force was to "develop guidelines that would reduce the potential for misuse of personal information and to avoid the loss of trust of consumers and library users"[2] as it pertains to the use of RFID technology. The task force released a policy statement in which it set out five RFID Privacy Principles:

1. Implement and enforce an up-to-date organizational privacy policy that gives notice and full disclosure as to the use, terms of use, and any change in the terms of use for data collected via new technologies and processes, including RFID.
2. Ensure that no personal information is recorded on RFID tags which, however, may contain a variety of transactional data.
3. Protect data by reasonable security safeguards against interpretation by any unauthorized third party.
4. Comply with relevant federal, state, and local laws as well as industry best practices and policies.
5. Ensure that the four principles outlined above must be verifiable by an independent audit.[3]

ALA Intellectual Freedom Committee Privacy and Confidentiality Guidelines (2005)

In 2005, the ALA's Intellectual Freedom Committee and the Office for Information Technology Policy developed "RFID in Libraries: Privacy and Confidentiality Guidelines" which were based on the work of a task force convened by the Book Industry Study Group but went further. The guidelines were adopted by ALA Council at ALA's 2005 Midwinter Meeting. The guidelines and best practices included:

1. Notify users about the library's use of RFID technology.
2. Label all RFID tag readers clearly so users know they are in use.
3. Protect the data on RFID tags by using encryption if available.
4. Limit the information stored on the RFID tag to a unique identifier or barcode.
5. Block the public from searching the catalog by the unique identifier.
6. Store no personally identifiable information on any RFID tag.[4]

NISO RFID Working Group Recommended Practices (2008)

In 2006, the NISO RFID Working Group on RFID in U.S. Libraries was formed to focus on the use and implementation of RFID technology in libraries. In 2008, the group formally published *RFID in U.S. Libraries*, a Recommended Practice of the National Information Standards Organization (NISO RP-6-2008).[5] The working group was composed of RFID vendors, software application providers, two librarians, and two BISG consultants. The document included recommended practices as well as a data model to facilitate interoperability between RFID vendors' solutions and also to facilitate use of the RFID tag across the entire life cycle of a book. Therefore, the proposed data model included fields for circulation, security, and ILL as well as fields that could be used by book publishers and others in the supply chain.

The first recommendation listed in this document was that tags should comply with the guidelines developed by the BISG working group, stating "in particular, ensuring that data relating to individual persons should never be recorded on item tags."[6] However, the document did not mention the best practices guidelines that had been adopted by ALA in 2005. In addition, the data model included options for including the owner library, shelf location, title, and "local data" fields and provided no mandates for how the local fields could be used. This caused some concern for privacy advocates.

Library Technology Reports Special Issue on Privacy, Chapter Six: "RFID in Libraries" (2010)

The November–December 2010 issue of *Library Technology Reports* focused on privacy and freedom of information. Deborah Caldwell-Stone authored chapter 6 focusing on RFID and privacy. In it, she states that the NISO recommendations and data model reflected the "needs of the commercial entities that make up the supply chain and not the needs and concerns of libraries and librarians."[7] She stated that librarians "should assume a leadership role in developing best practices and standards . . . for RFID as part of their ethical obligation to protect library users' privacy."[8]

NISO RFID Revision Working Group's Recommended Practice and US Data Profile for Public Comment (2011)

Also in 2010, a new NISO working group, the NISO RFID Revision Working Group, was formed to revise the 2008 NISO recommendations. The goals of the Revision Working Group were as follows:

- To review existing RFID standards, assess the applicability of this technology in U.S. libraries and across the book publishing supply chain, and promote the use of RFID where appropriate.
- To examine and assess privacy concerns associated with the adoption of RFID technologies in libraries.
- To investigate the way RFID may be used for the circulation or sale of books and other media in the United States and make recommendations.
- To focus on security and data models for RFID tags, along with issues of interoperability and privacy.
- To create a set of recommendations for libraries with regard to a tag data model and other issues, with the specific goals for this revision of:
    a. Reviewing and updating information in the original document.
    b. Ensuring conformance between the approved ISO standard and the NISO recommended practice.
    c. Creating a set of recommendations for a U.S. data model standard.
    d. Providing specific examples to make implementation easier for manufacturers and libraries.[9]

In April 2011, the group issued its revision for public comment. In this document, NISO recommended that the United States adopt ISO 28560-2 as the US Data Profile (application standard).

In the 2011 revision of the NISO recommendations, the Revision Working Group recommended that the US adopt ISO 28560-2 and provided guidelines for how to use each of the fields recommended for inclusion in the US Data Profile. The Working Group received "input from RFID hardware manufacturers, solution providers (software and integration), library RFID users, distributors, processors, and related organizations."[10] All participants in the supply chain (manufacturers, suppliers, distributors, libraries) had been taken into account, but the proposed standard applied primarily to libraries.

The revision refers to a checklist (for libraries and vendors) that can be used to evaluate the degree of conformance with the ISO 28560 standards,[11] a set of recommended practices and procedures to ensure interoperability among US RFID implementations, and a list of suggestions to reduce the impact of migrating from nonconforming systems to conforming systems.

NISO Finalizes US Data Profile—28560-2 (2012)

In March 2012, the RFID revision was adopted, thus establishing ISO 28560-2 as the US Data Profile. The final document was largely unchanged from the version released for comment. Both the revision and the final document included a description of all the data elements included in the data profile and made recommendations about how to use them.

The recommended practices were provided in order to promote procedures that would lead to installing the RFID early in the life cycle of the book. This way the tag could be used by publishers, distributors, and libraries (including for shelving, circulating, sorting, inventory, and security), as well as in interlibrary loan transactions. They also envisioned the tag being used in secondary markets such as secondhand books, returned books, and discarded or recycled books.

The hope is that the US Data Profile and associated recommendations will promote true interoperability between libraries. The Revision Working Group envisioned every library being able to use every other library's RFID tag regardless of the supplier, hardware, software, or ILS. They were attentive to the importance of protecting patron privacy while leveraging the technology. And they hoped the recommendations would lead to global interoperability and remain relevant and functional as the technology evolved.

The Revision Working Group supports most of the policy guidelines and best practices adopted by the ALA Intellectual Freedom Committee (IFC) in 2006; however, it does take issue with one recommendation. The IFC asserts that best practices dictate that only the barcode number should be stored on the tag. The Revision Working Group does not agree that only the barcode number should be stored on the tag. It does agree that no personally identifiable information should be stored on the tag, nor any transactional data regarding patron use.[12] The Group also suggests libraries blank out the Title and GS1-13 field if either has been used by upstream users (e.g., distributors).

While the Revision Working Group doesn't explicitly disagree with other IFC best practices, it would have been useful had it done so. For example, the IFC document encourages libraries to provide an RFID system from which a patron could "opt out." It isn't clear how this would protect patron privacy, because even if some patrons opted out (e.g., chose to use the barcode-only self check-out machines), the materials would still have RFID tags on them. The worry for privacy advocates is that someone will read the tag on a patron's in-circulation item, and using barcode-only equipment doesn't alleviate this concern.

Since 2006, the public's relationship to privacy has changed. Also, RFID technology has been widely adopted in many industries. And finally, with the latest standard, the AFI attribute is recommended. The AFI

Year	Libraries Worldwide Using RFID	US Library Activities	RFID Activities Worldwide
2003	100*	"RFID Technology for Libraries" (*Library Technology Reports*, Nov.–Dec. 2003) published.	ISO 15693 adopted. Walmart and Department of Defense request suppliers include RFID tags on pallets.
2004	>300†	BISC Policy Statement on RFID.	ISO 18000-3, Mode 1 adopted. FDA endorses use of RFID to combat drug counterfeiting.
2006		ALA IFC Privacy and Confidentiality Guidelines.	ISO 15692 Fixed Encoding Method (not library-specific) adopted. Gartner reports worldwide RFID spending expected to reach $504 million in 2005, $3 billion by 2010.‡
2006		Danish Data Model (DS/INF 163) for Libraries finalized.	EPC Gen2 standard finalized for UHF tags.
2007	600§		Defense Department stops requiring RFID tags on trucks and cargo; uses GPS and fleet management software instead.‖
2008		NISO RFID Working Group: Recommended Practice.	Gartner predicts worldwide RFID revenue will reach $1.2 billion in 2008; $3.5 billion by 2012.#
2009	1,500**		Worldwide RFID spending hits $5.56 billion.††
2011	2,400‡‡	ISO 28560 RFID for Libraries adopted. NISO tentatively recommends 28560-2 as US Data Profile.	IDTechEx predicts value of entire RFID market will be $5.84 billion in 2010.§§
2012	>3000‖	US Data Profile finalized.	IDTechEx report predicts 20 billion RFID tags annually will be required by apparel market alone within decade.##

* Richard Boss, "RFID Technology for Libraries," *Library Technology Reports* 39, no. 6 (November–December, 2003): 16. Boss reports that less than 200 libraries worldwide are using RFID. In his write-up on each of the RFID vendors including their customers, the list of US installations is well under 100.

† Scott Carlson, "Talking Tags," *Chronicle of Higher Education* 50, no. 48 (August 6, 2004): A29–A30. Over 300 in the US.

‡ Gartner, "Gartner Says Worldwide RFID Spending to Surpass $3 Billion in 2010" (news release), December 13, 2005, www.gartner.com/press_releases/asset_141469_11.html.

§ Richard Boss, "RFID Technology for Libraries," PLA Tech Notes, July 19, 2011, www.ala.org/pla/tools/technotes/rfidtechnology. Boss states, "By mid-2007, an estimated 600 libraries with as many as 850 facilities worldwide were using RFID systems. Those numbers had at least quadrupled by mid-2011 according to representatives of several companies contacted by the author."

‖ Sandra I Erwin, "Tracking Military Supplies No Longer Requires RFID," *National Defense* (online magazine), May 2007, www.nationaldefensemagazine.org/archive/2007/May/Pages/TrackingMilitary2637.aspx.

Gartner, "Gartner Says Worldwide RFID Revenue to Surpass $1.2 Billion in 2008" (news release), February 25, 2008, www.gartner.com/it/page.jsp?id=610807.

** Deborah Caldwell-Stone, "RFID in Libraries," chapter 6, in "Privacy and Freedom of Information in 21st-Century Libraries," *Library Technology Reports* 46, no. 8 (November–December 2010): 38. Caldwell-Stone states, "As of 2009, 1,500 libraries employ RFID applications in 2,500 facilities." Her source is an older version of the PLA Tech Note article "RFID Technology for Libraries" written by Richard Boss.

†† Peter Harrop, "RFID - Progress in Mid 2009," July 9, 2009, http://www.printedelectronicsworld.com/articles/rfid-progress-in-mid-2009-00001508.asp?sessionid=1.

‡‡ Boss, "RFID Technology for Libraries," PLA Tech Notes.

§§ Raghu Das and Peter Harrop, RFID Forecasts, Players and Opportunities 2011–2012 (Cambridge, MA: IDTechEx, 2011), www.idtechex.com/research/reports/rfid_forecasts_players_and_opportunities_2011_2021_000250.asp.

‖ "Description," in "RFID in Libraries," NXP website, www.nxp.com/applications/rf-identification/library.html#design-considerations. NXP states that over 3,000 libraries worldwide have introduced RFID to millions of customers.

Peter Harrop and Raghu Das, Apparel RFID 2011–2012 (Cambridge, MA: IDTechEx, January 2012), www.idtechex.com/research/reports/apparel-rfid-2011-2021-000256.asp.

Table 3.1
Timeline showing library and worldwide RFID activities.

attribute adds an additional level of protection against unauthorized reading of the tag by readers outside of the library industry.

It is time for the IFC to update the best practices document so that it provides implementable recommendations that do not simply restate the library's traditional approach to protecting patron privacy but that take into account the privacy protections patrons expect and desire today. And it is important that those who develop the best practices have a strong understanding of the benefits and limits of RFID technology in libraries.

Components of US Data Profile

There are many ways to implement ISO 28560-2. According to ISO 28560-2, only one field is mandatory, and the rest are optional. The ISO standard allows for some fields to be locked, and it provides some guidelines for how to use certain fields. When a field is locked, it cannot be changed. The advantage of locking a field is that it provides additional assurances that the tag data cannot be accidentally or intentionally modified. If a library has chosen to lock a field but then later needs to change the data, the tag will have to be replaced. The Data Profile includes specific recommendations for how the ISO standard should be implemented in the United States and when fields should or should not be locked.

Mandatory Data Elements

The US Data Profile includes two mandatory data elements: Primary Object ID (i.e., barcode) and Tag Content Key. The field Owner Library is also recommended. The reason Owner Library is recommended is that the combination of the Primary Object ID with the Owner Library provides for a nationally (and possibly globally) unique item identifier. This has ramifications for how the tags could be used to support ILL and resource-sharing workflows. The UK Data Profile, also based on ISO 28560-2, makes Owner Library mandatory (this is the only difference between the US and UK Data Profiles).

By limiting the mandatory fields to just the barcode number and tag content key, the Revision Working Group provided a way for libraries to continue to use the tags much like they do today. This minimalist approach provides an acceptable way forward for libraries for whom patron privacy concerns are paramount.

Optional Data Elements

There are 22 optional elements included in the US Profile (see table 3.2 for complete list). Two of the fields included in ISO 28560-2 have been excluded from the US Data Profile. These are MARC Media Format (in favor of the ONIX Media Format field) and Supplier Invoice Number (although Supplier Identifier and Order Number were included).

Fields Using ISIL Codes

Owner Library and ILL Borrowing Institution refer to ISIL codes. The ISIL Registration Authority will issue US libraries an ISIL code for the purposes of using the code on RFID tags. Alternatively, an OCLC code could be used, as these are ISIL-compatible. If the Owning Library or ILL Borrowing Institutions do not have an ISIL or ISIL-compatible code, the standard states that the Alternative Owner Library and Alternative ILL Borrowing Institution fields should be used instead.

Set Info

Set Info allows the library to encode information about multipart sets onto the tag. The field contains the total number of items in the set and the part number of the item to which the tag is affixed. Some libraries are already taking advantage of this data element.

Type of Usage

Type of Usage is a field that provides additional information about the intended use of the item. For example, an item can be tagged as a circulating item or as reference material or as adult material (e.g., R-rated movie). Using the tag this way would allow the circulation and security system to prevent a patron from checking out a reference book while the ILS was down or a teen from checking out an R-rated movie.

Title

It is unfortunate that the proposed data profile doesn't specify that Title should remain unlocked. If locked, information about the content of the tagged item is stored on the tag Title. None of the other fields contain any personally identifying information or even specific information about the content of the item, so even if they were locked, it wouldn't pose a particular privacy concern. Title, however, is a field that many libraries would choose to leave blank once an item goes into circulation.

UCC/ISBN/ISSN

Another field, GS1-13, raises the same concerns as Title. GS1-13, or the UCC Code, as it is known in the United States, can be used for the ISBN or ISSN by pre-pending "978" or "979" (ISBN) or "977" (ISSN) to the number. ISBNs are easy enough to associate with a particular title. While some libraries might want to use this field to provide additional services for patrons, many others will insist that this field be left blank on circulating material. Specifying that this field remain unlocked would have provided support for this latter group.

The ISBN could be used in interesting ways for library patrons. For example, electronic reader's advisory services can be provided based on the ISBN. Recommendations could be provided to patrons based on items they are checking out or returning or perhaps

Field	Category	Purpose/Codes	Locking
Primary Item ID	Mandatory	Item identification	Optional
Tag Content Key	Mandatory	Determining what other data is on the tag	No
Owner Library	Optional	Use ISIL Code (see ISO 15511)	Optional
Set Info	Optional	Item properties	Optional
Type of Usage	Optional	Coded list of type of item usage	Optional
Shelf Location	Optional	To support inventory (LC or Dewey call number)	Optional
ONIX Media Format	Optional	Item properties (ONIX code list)	Optional
Supplier Identifier	Optional	Acquisitions processing	Not recommended
Order Number	Optional	Acquisitions processing	Not recommended
ILL Borrowing Institution	Optional	Use ISIL Code (see ISO 15511)	No
ILL Borrowing Transaction ID	Optional	ILL transaction tracking	No
GS1-13 (UCC and ISBN)	Optional	Identification	Optional
Alternative unique item identifier (reserved)	Optional but should not be used until defined by ISO 28560	Identification	Not recommended
Local Data—A	Optional	For local or regional use	Optional
Local Data—B	Optional	For local or regional use	Optional
Title	Optional	Identification	Optional
Product Identifier (local)	Optional	Identification	Optional
Media Format	Optional	Item properties (no code list defined)	Optional
Supply Chain Stage	Optional	For multi-use (coded list)	No
Alternative Item Identifier	Optional	Item identification	Optional
Alternative Owner Library Identifier	Optional	Item identification (for codes not ISIL compliant)	Optional
Subsidiary of Owner Library	Optional	Item Identification	Optional
Alternative ILL Borrowing Institution	Optional	Support for ILL for non-ISIL code	No
Local Data—C	Optional	For local or regional use	Optional

Table 3.2
Fields included in US Data Profile based on ISO 28560, *RFID in U.S. Libraries.*

at a special Get Recommendations kiosk that could be used to find another book like the one they'd just enjoyed reading.

Each library will need to find the right balance between patron privacy concerns and providing convenient and expansive library services. The trend has been toward more convenience with much less concern about privacy, but this varies quite a bit from community to community.[13]

Shelf Location

The Shelf Location field can be used to specify where an item should be shelved. In addition to encoding the actual LC or Dewey number in this field, the library could also specify Adult Fiction or Entrance Display in this field. This field could be useful when sorting material based on information on the RFID tag. For example, the sorter could be programmed to sort all Adult Fiction to one bin and Entrance Display to another. While this is possible already, it requires the sorter to communicate with the ILS. With the information on the RFID tag, the additional sorting granularity could be accomplished independent of an ILS connection.

Fields Supporting Receiving Processing

Supplier Identifier and Order Number could contain data useful in the receiving functions of a library. If these fields are used, new items arriving at the library could be received without needing to individually scan each item. This would dramatically improve the receiving workflows in the library's technical services department.

Many libraries are already using EDI (electronic data interchange) in their workflows. EDI allows items to be ordered and invoiced electronically. Theoretically, receiving can also be performed electronically, but it is usually implemented last (if at all). This is partly because libraries often receive partial orders and also because they feel more confident verifying that the packing slip actually matches what is in the shipment. Libraries are more comfortable unpacking the box, scanning in each item as received, and putting it on a book cart.

Using Supplier Identifier and Order Number, the library could receive all items in a box and verify the contents without actually having to handle each item or even opening the box. An RFID tunnel is a piece of equipment designed for this purpose and it is common outside of the United States. Only recently has one RFID vendor included an RFID tunnel in its product line for sale to US libraries.

Fields Supporting ILL Processing

Using ILL Borrowing Institution and ILL Borrowing Transaction ID could eliminate much of the paperwork and labor associated with performing ILL transactions. The ILL Borrowing Institution (perhaps in combination with other fields) can be used in sorting systems to route outbound ILL items to the appropriate delivery route and location (if part of a closed delivery system) or to the shipping department if the item needs to be sent out via a shipping service.

The ILL Borrowing Transaction ID represents the key to the entire ILL transaction in terms of both the borrowing and lending libraries' workflow. Whatever ILL software is used to initiate the transaction, the data is associated with a transaction ID. By writing that transaction ID to the tag, each library is freed from filling out paperwork that needs to travel with the item. Referencing the transaction ID in the shared ILL software would simply pull up all the pertinent information.

Local Data Fields

The proposed profile also includes three Local Data fields. These fields are there to provide even more flexibility for the library. The data model does not specify the size of these fields, so the library can really use them in whatever way it likes.

Supply Chain Stage

Many people involved in library RFID (this author included) hope to see tags placed in new items at the manufacturer stage so that they can be used for multiple purposes along the way. The Supply Chain Stage field exists to support this vision. Once an item becomes a library item, this field would be encoded with "64." The data model defines other numbers that are associated with other stages including manufacturer (16), publisher (24), distributor (32), and jobber (48). This field is used so that fields can be interpreted correctly depending on where they are in the supply chain. For example, the Primary Item Identifier in a library is the library's barcode number. However, a book distributor may encode the EPC code as the Primary Identifier.

Subsidiary of an Owner Library

This field is to be used in addition to the Owner Institution field (or Alternative Owner Institution field). It does not use ISIL or ISIL-compatible codes. It can be a short alphanumeric string to identify individual outlets associated with a library. The expectation is that this field will be used to identify home branches for material owned by the Owner Institution. This field could also be used to support floating or rotating collections management.

Notes

1. NISO RFID Revision Working Group, *RFID in U.S. Libraries,* Recommended Practice of the National Information Standards Organization, NISO RP-6-2012 (Baltimore, MD: NISO, March 2012), v, www.niso.org/apps/group_public/download.php/8269/RP-6-2012_RFID-in_US_Libraries.pdf.
2. Book Industry Study Group, *Radio Frequency Identification,* BISG Policy Statement POL-002 (New York: BISG, September 2004), 1.
3. Ibid., 2.
4. See "RFID in Libraries: Privacy and Confidentiality Guidelines," www.ala.org/offices/oif/statementspols/otherpolicies/rfidguidelines.
5. NISO RFID Working Group, *RFID in U.S. Libraries,* Recommended Practice of the National Information Standards Organization, NISO RP-6-2008 (Baltimore, MD: NISO, December 2007), www.niso.org/publications/rp/RP-6-2008.pdf.
6. Ibid., viii.
7. Deborah Caldwell-Stone, "RFID in Libraries," chapter 6, in "Privacy and Freedom of Information in 21st-Century Libraries," *Library Technology Reports* 46, no. 8 (November–December 2010): 42.
8. Ibid.
9. NISO RFID Revision Working Group, *RFID in U.S. Libraries,* Recommended Practice of the National Information Standards Organization, NISO RP-6-201x, draft for public comment (Baltimore, MD: NISO, April 2011), iv, www.niso.org/apps/group_public/download.php?document_id=6508.
10. Ibid.
11. Ibid. The checklist is available from http://biblstandard.dk/rfid/docs/conformance_28560-2.pdf.
12. See section 6, "Privacy," in NISO RFID Revision Working Group, *RFID in U.S. Libraries* (March 2012), 36–38.
13. Anita L. Allen, *Unpopular Privacy: What Must We Hide* (New York: Oxford University Press, 2011).

Chapter 4

Moving Your RFID System to the New US Data Profile

Abstract

Chapter 4 of Library Technology Reports *(vol. 48, no. 5) "RFID in Libraries: A Step toward Interoperability" discusses moving RFID to the new US Data Profile. It will take a concerted effort to move from a library's existing RFID system to one that is compliant with the new standards. However, in order to achieve interoperability and to extend the uses of RFID in libraries, libraries need to do just that. This chapter provides recommendations for libraries that already have RFID installed and those that are looking to get started. It also discusses how RFID technology can be leveraged beyond basic circulation and security functions to do much more.*

There are many decisions for a library to make when it already has an RFID system in place (see figure 4.1). The first question to ask is "What are the benefits of complying with the new standard?" It may not be worthwhile for some libraries to immediately migrate from a noncompliant RFID solution if they are supported by a reputable vendor, their system is working, and they do not participate actively in resource sharing. If this is the case, it may not make sense to convert the existing tags. However, even for libraries that are not compelled to migrate their already-tagged material to the new standard, it is worth moving to a standard tag and the new data profile for all new acquisitions. Reputable RFID vendors will work with their library customers to find a way to introduce the new tags into the workflow and provide hardware upgrades as needed to support a mixed environment (more than one data model encoded on ISO-compliant tags).

Because ISO 18000-3 has been the accepted standard for the physical tag, most libraries have compliant tags. Only the very early adopters have noncompliant tags. Replacing noncompliant tags doesn't really work because of the damage removing the tag causes to library material. What generally happens is that a new, compliant tag is added. This approach also creates some problems. Tags that overlap interfere with each other, so finding a location on the library item where there will be no interference is sometimes difficult. Some libraries have found that they needed to cut the antenna on the old tags to eliminate the interference problems (regardless of where the new tags were placed).

If the existing tags are compliant tags, there may still be challenges ahead. If any of the fields on the encoded tag are locked, it may prevent the tag from being rewritten using the new data model. The only way to migrate these items to the new standard would be to replace the tags (or add a new, compliant tag to the item).

The way security is implemented on a library's existing RFID system will be an important issue to resolve. The standard strongly recommends implementing AFI (application family identifier), which provides several benefits, one of which is that it can be used for security. The purpose of the AFI is to prevent tags from different industries from interfering with each other. The AFI is used to identify an item as part of a "family" or industry (e.g., a library book is in the "library" family, and a book on the shelf at Barnes & Noble is in the "retail" family). Each industry has been allocated a set of unique values. In the library industry, two values are specified. AFI value C2 indicates the item is in the "library" family and it is checked out (unsecured). AFI value O7 indicates the item is in the "library" family and is checked in (secured).

Security gates can read the AFI value to determine whether to set off the alarms or not. The placement of

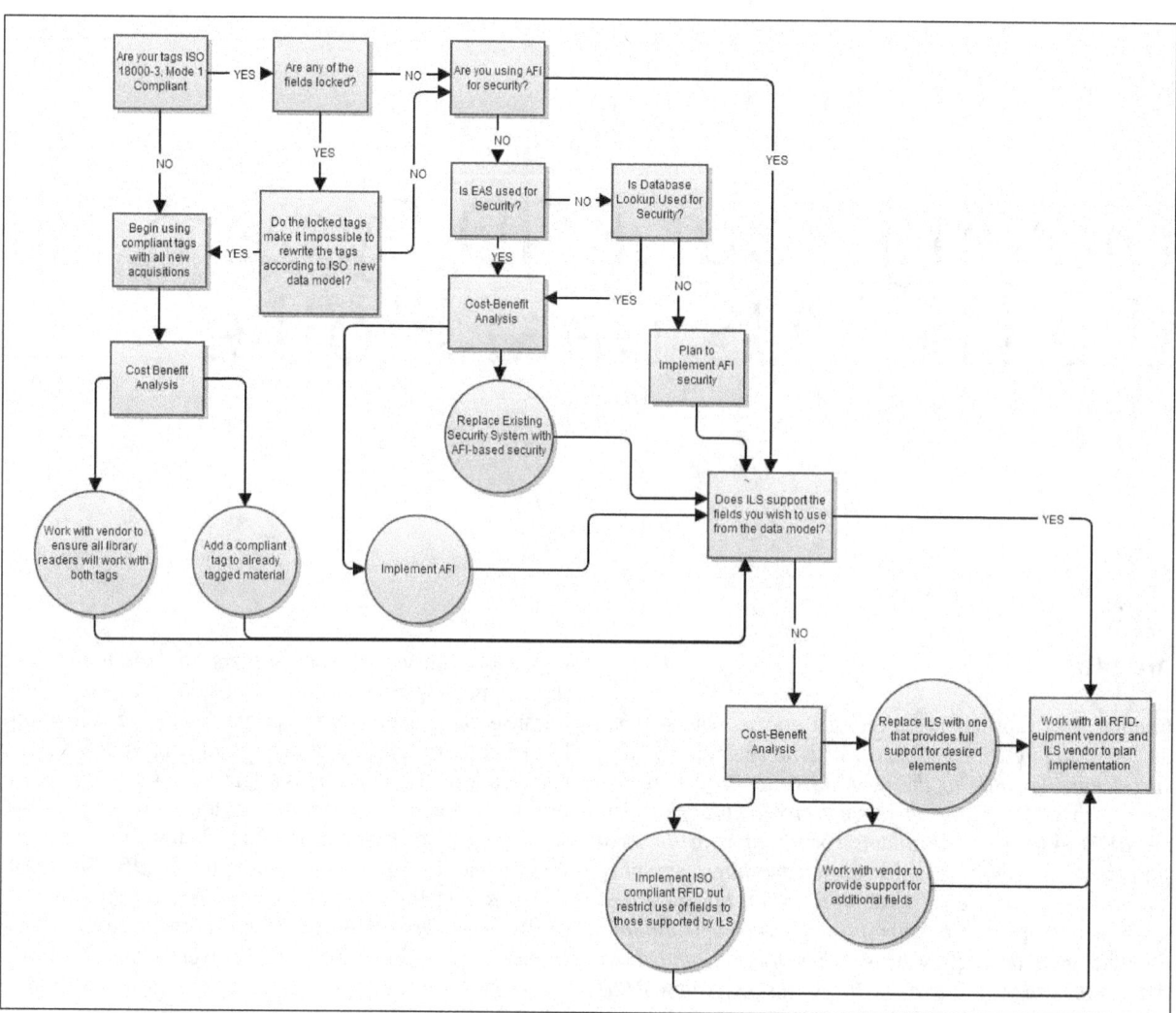

Figure 4.1
Flowchart showing decision points for upgrading current RFID system to new standard.

the AFI on the chip does not vary depending on which data model is employed, so any security gates can read it. For this reason, the AFI can be used to manage item-level security of another library's items. In other words, at least as far as security is concerned, using the AFI attribute for security provides the potential for interoperability between library security systems.

An important reason to use the AFI is that it ensures that library tags can't be read by nonlibrary readers. It also ensures that library tags will not interfere with other nonlibrary readers. For this reason, the current US standard specifies that the AFI should be set, even if it is not used for library security.

If the library is using EAS (Electronic Article Surveillance) or database look-up for security, it may need to work with its vendor to implement AFI in addition to, or instead of, its existing security system.

Libraries will also need to work with their RFID vendors as well as their ILS vendors to determine what can be supported in terms of data elements. Communication between the ILS and the RFID equipment relies on the protocols supported, and interfaces provided, by the ILS. SIP2 is supported to some degree by most ILS vendors. NCIP and NCIP2 are supported by some ILS vendors. However, neither of these protocols provides support for all the data elements available in the US Data Profile. As a result, leveraging the compliant tags and the new data profile will take time and require libraries to work with their ILS vendors to demand the support they need.

Considerations for New RFID Implementations

Once the US Data Profile is adopted and implemented throughout US libraries and by RFID vendors, libraries will be able to confidently purchase RFID tags and equipment from any vendor, and security systems will work consistently as material moves from library to library and system to system. Over time, ILS vendors and RFID equipment vendors will provide support for more of the profile's data elements, and libraries will begin thinking differently about their workflows and how they can use their RFID tags to optimize the workflows and work more efficiently. The sooner libraries insist on compliant tags and systems, the sooner the prices for tags and equipment will come down. Without vendor lock-in and proprietary solutions, RFID equipment and supplies will be more competitively priced. It will be a good time to begin planning a new RFID implementation.

Choose RFID Components Rather Than an RFID Vendor

The beauty of having standards is that once everyone follows them, we can mix and match products that rely on the RFID tags. The RFID system no longer has to determine the library's materials handling or self-service fate. Libraries can choose the best products from among the array of vendor choices as long as the tags are ISO 18000-3, Mode 1 tags and each vendor encodes the tags according to the US Data Profile.

Before the ISO 28560 standards were finalized, libraries tended to choose an RFID vendor rather than RFID components. This was the best way to ensure that all the pieces would work together. However, this approach doesn't necessarily get the library the best solution. This is particularly apparent when considering automated materials handling (AMH) solutions because some excellent AMH vendors are not in the RFID business. They sell sorters and self check-in machines and maybe self check-out machines, but their systems are agnostic on the matter of barcodes or RFID tags, and they do not provide RFID solutions as part of their business model. Many libraries have issued single tenders for an "RFID and AMH system" and found that certain companies didn't respond to the RFP because that vendor couldn't provide the total solution. With a US Data Profile providing the standards, it is no longer necessary to do one-stop shopping.

Even among the RFID vendor offerings, there is reason to mix and match. For example, some RFID staff interfaces work better with one ILS than others. But just because the staff workstation from one vendor is better doesn't mean that vendor's self-check machines are superior. As long as the library specifies that all tags and equipment must comply with the new standard, the equipment should be interoperable.

Choosing Tags

Although the tags themselves are manufactured by only a few companies, libraries can purchase them from any number of vendors as well as consortia. They can be purchased from library supply companies, companies that provide RFID staff equipment, security gates, or self-check equipment, the AMH vendor, or the library's book supplier.

However, purchasing tags from established library vendors has some advantages. In most cases, the vendors will guarantee the tag for the life of the item to which it is affixed. Whether this warranty is provided by the manufacturer or not, the library RFID vendors often agree to replace any tags that need to be replaced on a book, CD, or DVD. They are counting on the relatively short circulating lifespan of the library item compared to the lifespan of the tag. Once placed inside a book or on a CD or DVD, the tags are expected to function very effectively for ten years or more.

However, libraries shouldn't rely just on the expectation that the tags will continue to work effectively for the life of their library items. In rare cases, some tags have been found to lose read range over time. This may be something that is largely addressed with state-of-the-art ISO 18000-3, Mode 1 tags, but libraries are advised to establish clear criteria for what it means to warrant the tag for the life of the book. Does it mean guaranteeing the tag won't fall off?—in which case, that is really just a warranty on the adhesive used.

The quality guarantee with your tag provider should include guarantees of the tags' effectiveness in numerous ways:

- Does the tag stay attached to the item and not interfere with its operation (e.g., the CD/DVD tags). Whether your library is in Alaska or the Bahamas, the tag should stay attached.
- Does the read range degrade over time, or does it stay consistent for the life of the item? Measure the read range of the tags in various situations in your library and document their effectiveness. Use that as the measure that you and your tag supplier will use to determine if there is any degradation.
- Are bit dropouts causing problems reading and writing the data accurately? Unfortunately, it isn't possible to use error correction with the 28560-2 standard, so if some of the bits encoded on the tag begin randomly changing (as can happen with these kinds of electronics), you could start having a lot of trouble using your equipment. With high-quality tags, bit dropout is likely to be rare and isolated. But there is always the chance of getting a bad batch, so including a way to get those tags replaced is a contingency that should be written into your warranty.

As of this writing, standard book tags were available for under 20 cents each. Full-coverage CD/DVD tags range from 65 cents to 91 cents each, but look for the price of these tags to go down as more libraries start using the full-coverage tags instead of the ring tags.

Tagging New Acquisitions

Once the library decides to move forward with RFID, it will want to get the RFID tags in place as early in the workflow as possible. Book jobbers will provide the RFID tag in new material, but eventually, industry experts expect that RFID tags will be installed at manufacture.

Purchasing new library material with tags already in place is a great way to optimize the library's technical services workflow. Most jobbers such as Baker & Taylor, Midwest Tape, and Ingram can put pre-encoded (with the barcode number) RFID tags inside the material they provide to libraries. With a data model standard, it will be easier for the jobbers to provide this service because the variations between library data profiles and proprietary encoding methods will be largely eliminated. This should bring down the cost of providing these services and therefore the fees charged to libraries.

Libraries can also install RFID tags on new material as part of their technical services workflow. However, it is likely that eventually tags will be provided in all new library material, so this particular workflow may be short-lived. Let's hope so.

Tagging the Existing Collection (Retrospective Conversion)

Whether outsourcing or doing the tagging with library staff (see the section Tagging Costs in chapter 2 for more information on these two options), the following guidelines should be followed to ensure your RFID conversion process meets the US Data Profile standard:

1. Use ISO 18000-3, Mode 1 tags.
2. Encode the tags according to ISO 28560-2.
3. Stagger the placement of tags inside the material.

The first step is to buy the correct type of tag and the standard that related to the physical tag is ISO 18000-3, Mode 1. What you write on that tag and how you encode it is a function of the ISO 28560 standards and the finalized US Data Profile is based on those ISO 28560 standards.

Deciding How to Use the Data Elements

Most RFID implementations today encode only the barcode number and maybe some set information to their RFID tag. However, the data elements provided by the new standards create opportunities to improve some of the more labor-intensive workflows. To take advantage of these elements, the library needs to do the work to rethink its workflows and then get the cooperation of several key players, including the ILS vendor and the manufacturers of the RFID-enabled equipment.

One of the first decisions to be made is what data should be stored on the tag and what data should be stored in the ILS. Traditionally, all information about a library item, patron, and transaction has been stored in the ILS. Information that will enhance the library's operation or allows the library to function when connectivity to the ILS is unavailable may be a good candidate for storing on the tag. For example:

- Use Type of Usage to ensure noncirculating material isn't checked out.
- Use Destination Library to sort material at off-site sorting facilities and eliminate the need for routing slips.
- Use Supplier Identifier and Order Number to enhance receiving operations.
- Use Set Information to enhance security of multipart sets.

The RFID Opportunity for Libraries

With the release of the US Data Profile, libraries are finally in a position to fully commit to library RFID. Libraries can purchase tags that won't need to be replaced due to new standards, and by following the US Data Profile standard, they can be assured that equipment from any vendor will be compatible with their existing equipment and tags. As more and more libraries migrate their RFID systems to the standard, tags from one library can be used in other libraries for both identification and security. Gradually, additional functionality will be supported as others in the supply chain adopt the standard and as the ILS vendors develop interfaces that support the new possibilities.

The final adoption of a US Data Profile is one big step toward interoperability between libraries and between vendors. However, there are still several more steps to be taken before libraries can avail themselves of the additional opportunities RFID technology provides. These additional steps are to remove any legacy barriers to interoperability, develop a mechanism for verifying compliance, envision new uses for RFID, and extend ILS support for the new uses.

Remove Legacy Barriers to Interoperability

There are still potential barriers to interoperability even with the new standard. These come in the name of "enhancements" that might be offered by vendors. Vendors will surely seek ways to differentiate their products now that their proprietary solutions have been "end-of-lifed" with the new standards. These enhancements may appear attractive to libraries that don't understand that using these enhancements will render their systems noninteroperable with other libraries or other vendors. They may be attracted to

> *An important reason to use the AFI is that it ensures that library tags can't be read by nonlibrary readers. It also ensures that library tags will not interfere with other nonlibrary readers. For this reason, the current US standard specifies that the AFI should be set, even if it is not used for library security.*

the promise of better security or improved privacy protections that the enhancements offer. Some libraries may have legitimate reasons to seek these enhancements, but it is important to recognize which features will affect the interoperability of your RFID system because this will increasingly be a big cost to pay as more and more libraries rely on the ability to use each other's tags. It's very possible that eventually RFID tags will be as critical to library operations as the barcode is today.

Some of the enhancements that could interfere with the interoperability of a library's heretofore-compliant RFID system are:

- Vendor-specific encrypting and encoding of the data
- Proprietary security functions
- Software or firmware that is system dependent and can only be used with specific tags

When designing your library's RFID system and working with vendors, be sure to remain cognizant of the effect of any decisions you make on the interoperability of your system. Moving from interoperable to proprietary puts the library in a dangerous and potentially expensive position that is probably not worth whatever the so-called enhancements are.

Developing a Mechanism for Verifying Compliance

Related to the above barrier is the need to develop a mechanism for US libraries to verify that the tags they are purchasing are compliant, that the library's implementation of the data model is compliant, and that each vendor writing to the tags is doing so consistent with the library's data model and the standard.

As of this writing, there is no mechanism for doing any of these things in the United States. It is important that libraries have a way to ensure compliance that goes beyond vendor assurances. As we know from past experiences, vendors do not always know when they are compliant. The standard provides for a lot of flexibility for the library (in terms of which fields it will use) and for the vendors that write data to the tags. Encoding data on the tag is a complex business[1] that involves writing data to different areas of the tag, encoding the data elements, and compacting the data.

Convergent Software is a company located in the United Kingdom. It has developed a set of tools that can be used by vendors and libraries to verify compliance to ISO 28560-2. The United Kingdom and Australia both adopted ISO 28560-2 long before NISO began moving in that direction, so the development of these tools in the United Kingdom is no surprise. However, it remains to be seen how US libraries can avail themselves of these tools. It isn't reasonable for every library implementing a compliant RFID system to purchase this company's tools to verify compliance. The tools are not trivial in terms of ease of use or cost. However, neither is it reasonable to trust vendors to verify their own system whether they use this particular company's tools or not.

Moving forward, US libraries need to identify a mechanism for verifying compliance that is affordable for libraries. The service must be offered by an objective third party (not an RFID vendor). The service needs to be available to libraries to test a vendor's tags (before and after encoding) and to assist libraries in developing their own compliant implementation plan. Whether this role is appropriate for a NISO body, ALA, or an independent entrepreneur is for the library community to decide. But it is important to begin discussing the issue of verifying compliance.

Envision New Uses for RFID

Until a few years ago, the push for RFID has come largely from vendors interested in selling RFID tags. Like every other industry using RFID tags, the library needs to determine how to leverage this technology rather than use it in a limited way. Prior to the finalization of the US Data Profile, it is understandable that libraries were reluctant to move in any direction about extending the use of RFID. Library RFID tags contain the barcode number and not much more. But the potential for doing much more is now here. It is up to libraries to decide how to take advantage of the tags to optimize workflows for staff and patrons and provide new services for patrons. For example:

- Use Set Info to improve security of multipart sets.
- Eliminate the use of routing slips in libraries by using Owner Library, ILL Borrowing Institution and possibly Subsidiary of an Owner Library, and Shelf Location to sort material. The library system's sort facilities could be equipped with

RFID-based sorters (human or automated) capable of sorting material without either routing slips or a connection to the ILS. The United Kingdom and the Danes are already using Owner Library and ILL Borrowing Institution this way.
- Develop a library app for RFID-enabled smartphones that allow users to check out items with their phones, eliminating the need to stop at a self-check machine to turn off security at a special kiosk. (Tech-Logic/Boopsie currently support self-checkout with a user's smartphone, but it requires turning off security at a special kiosk.)
- Use UCC, ISBN, or ISSN umbers on noncirculating items that work with RFID-enabled smartphones and library-developed apps that link to enhanced content such as reviews or recommendations.
- Use of Type of Usage to provide better control of items when the ILS is down.
- Use Title on noncirculating items to provide support for mobile devices that could help staff and perhaps even patrons locate specific items.
- Set up reader's advisory kiosks in the library or vending machines in other locations that can be used to find "more books like this one" while accepting returns.
- Use Shelf Location to provide more granular sorting of returned items to more quickly move items back to the Hold shelf or display area or up to the third floor.
- Receive new acquisitions box by box instead of item by item using Supplier Identifier and Order Number in combination with the unique identifier on each new item.
- Eliminate much of the paperwork involved in ILL processing by encoding the ILL transaction number on the tag and using the ILL or ILS software to track the transaction.
- Use a Local Data field to count circulations or "date last circulated" to support weeding functions without requiring a connection to the ILS.
- Use a Local Data field to indicate special handling requirements for items in the back office.

The possibilities are endless, but to take advantage of those possibilities, people working in libraries need to understand how the technology works and then start thinking creatively. Rather than waiting for the vendors to come up with some ideas that they think are marketable, the push for new developments should really come from library staff and library users themselves.

Extend ILS Support for RFID

With a set of defined fields libraries can use and standards to ensure we can use those fields while still being assured of library and vendor interoperability, all that is holding us back is our own creativity and ILS support. In order for RFID vendors to work with the ILS, they need to be able to communicate—to pass information back and forth. At the present time, there are two established protocols for supporting communication with the ILS: SIP and NCIP.

SIP and NCIP

SIP was originally designed by 3M to support its self-check machines. In 1993, 3M released SIP 1.0 so that ILS vendors and self-service vendors could all use the same protocol. In 2006, SIP2 was released with additional capabilities. Today, virtually all ILS systems provide support for SIP2. SIP2 has been extended beyond simply self-check, but not a lot farther. SIP2 supports a fairly limited range of activities: look up patron status; get patron information; check items in and out; renew items; create, modify, and delete holds; get item information.[2]

Although SIP2 is the most widely adopted ILS communication protocol available, SIP2 support means very different things from one vendor to the next. One can claim to be SIP2-compliant without supporting all of the message pairs available in the protocol. In fact, some vendors have developed SIP extensions that go beyond the specified message pairs in order to provide for more expansive communication with the ILS. These extensions weakened the usefulness of SIP2 as the de facto standard, but there weren't any better alternatives at the time.[3]

NCIP was another protocol that many hoped would replace SIP2. It was conceived of as a more robust ILS communication protocol than SIP2. NCIP, version 1.0, was released in 2002 but didn't catch on partly because of how it was written. Communications using NCIP 1.0 were slow and very difficult for ILS vendors to implement. As of version 2.0, released in 2008, NCIP has slowly gained ground. It is the key protocol for supporting resource-sharing handling communications related to traditional interlibrary loans as well as direct consortial borrowing. In addition, it handles many of the same messages that SIP2 supports.[4]

Between SIP2 and NCIP2, third-party providers can communicate with the ILS to perform most circulation functions. However, many of the capabilities made possible by RFID, described earlier in this paper, remain unsupported by SIP2 and NCIP2.

In January 2012, SIP3 was announced. SIP3 provides several new messages and support for additional functionality. However, SIP3 still focuses primarily on circulation and doesn't really address the issue of RFID specifically.

BIC and BLCF

Libraries in the United Kingdom have been two steps ahead of the United States as it pertains to RFID. In

2009, a well-respected library RFID consultant, Mick Fortune, posted a message on his blog that articulates many of the points made in this paper.[5] At that time, he announced that the United Kingdom had adopted ISO 28560-2 as the UK Data Model and explained to his readers that they would no longer need to buy all their "RFID toys from the same toyshop" (vendor interoperability). He explained the benefits of being able to identify ILL items circulating around the country via the RFID tags (library interoperability). And he encouraged libraries to begin thinking about how to use the tags more expansively.

Between 2009 and today, Mick Fortune has been working with UK libraries to ensure that their RFID systems are interoperable. He's working on developing mechanisms for ensuring compliance, and he's encouraging libraries to insist on better ILS communication protocols so that the power of RFID can finally be harnessed.

The Book Industry Communication (BIC) is an independent UK organization set up and sponsored by the Publishers Association, Booksellers Association, Chartered Institute of Library and Information Professionals (CILIP), and the British Library. Its purpose is to promote supply-chain efficiency in all sectors of the book world through e-commerce and the application of standard processes and procedures.

In January 2011, BIC announced plans to develop a new communications framework to improve communications between the ILS and RFID systems. In March 2011, a first draft was published which "replicates and extends the range of activities commonly conducted using 3M's open SIP2 protocol and additionally provides web services functionality for the exchange of information."[6]

The BIC Library Communications Framework (BLCF)

Version 0.9 of the BIC Library Communications Framework was released in March 2011.[7] The BLCF does several things that SIP2 (and the just released SIP3) do not:

- BLCF provides support for Web services.
- BLCF is designed to be further developed by BIC rather than being managed and owned by a single vendor.
- BLCF is compatible with SIP2 and some existing APIs.
- BLCF is not limited to serial communications.
- BLCF provides support for ISO 28560 data elements.

There are many reasons to like BLCF. It doesn't seek to replace SIP. According to Fortune, one could argue that SIP2 and SIP3 are simply implementations of BLCF. Another revision of SIP (e.g., SIP4) could take advantage of the fact that BLCF identifies all of the known data pairs, and the possible values, that might need to be exchanged between the ILS and any client application.[8]

BLCF provides a thoughtful framework for moving beyond SIP to a set of protocols and standards that utilize a technology that allows for reading multiple items at once (rather than protocols based on the one-at-a-time nature of barcode-based communication).

BLCF provides a roadmap to move toward protocols and standards that fully support RFID. Until these standards and protocols are developed, each RFID vendor must use its own proprietary means of communicating information to support activities unaddressed by SIP2, SIP3, or NCIP2. BLCF is a framework for standardizing communications that support many basic RFID activities such as shelf reading, inventory, locating lost items, pulling items, and much more.

As Jim Hopwood, CTO of Bibliotheca, states, "Having a framework like BLCF will mean that new opportunities and products can be developed with the knowledge that they can be integrated with a wide variety of systems, without having to resort to proprietary interfaces. To libraries, this means they can implement new technology without fearing lock-in and obsolescence."[9]

Other RFID Technologies in Libraries

NFC-Enabled Smartphones

NFC (near field communication) is a type of RFID that operates in the 13.56 MHz spectrum (making it HF, like our library tags). But unlike our library tags, which can be read up to 18 inches away, NFC chips require the reader to be no further away than an inch. This proximity requirement is the key to their security. The standards that apply to NFC (contactless) are different from the library standards (item management), so although they are based on the same technology and operate in the same spectrum, they are really a whole different beast.

There are three categories of NFC applications (so far). They are service initiation, where the technology is used to "unlock" another service (think of QR codes without having to open a QR reading application); peer-to-peer, where NFC is used to enable communication between two devices (think Bluetooth, but easier to use and requiring the two devices to be very close); and payment and ticketing (Google Wallet being the most obvious example).

The holy grail of NFC is payment systems. So all the stars have to align to get it going: smartphone manufacturers, banks, and the telecom companies. Google Wallet is backed by Citibank, Sprint, and MasterCard. And of course, it requires your Android phone. You can use your Google Wallet in Walgreens, Subway, and Macy's today. To pay for something, you simply hold your phone up to the reader and enter your PIN.[10]

Some predicted that we'd all be paying with our smartphones by now, but there have been a couple of stumbling blocks. While Google Wallet was the first one to debut NFC-enabled payment systems, there is a competitor to Google called Isis, which is a joint venture of Verizon, AT&T, and T-Mobile USA.[11]

Whether one service will win out or both will gain traction will become clearer in 2012. At any rate, libraries should get ready to accept payment for fines and fees by 2013.[12]

NFC and Library Cards

Library cards will likely change in two ways as a result of NFC. One option is for libraries to NFC-enable the library cards they provide to their patrons. The cards could be used in all those places where patrons now have to type in their 15-digit barcode number. This would require an NFC reader to be provided at each such location. While it might be wonderfully convenient for the patron, it might be a bit expensive for libraries.

The more likely change is that library cards will be something that virtually live on your NFC-enabled smartphone just as all of your credit cards will. Patrons will be able to pay fines and fees with their smartphone as well as sign up for programs, reserve meeting rooms, begin their self-check transaction, and get access to various types of content from the NFC tags libraries will embed in posters, at exhibits, on doors, and maybe even in library material. The doors may even unlock themselves when the right smartphone comes along.

UHF and Asset Tracking

When the EPC Gen 2 standard was finalized for UHF RFID tags, several industries leaped on the tags and began developing new applications with them. One application that libraries should be paying attention to is asset tracking. Like the library RFID systems we've been talking about so far, this type of RFID application is composed of tags, readers, and some kind of application.

UHF RFID tags are the preferred type of tag to use for this purpose because the goal is to quickly detect everything in an area such as all the IT assets in a room or office. The types of assets that might be tagged are computers, laptops, servers, routers, projectors, furniture, printers, and other equipment. A wide range of UHF tags are available for asset tracking. Which ones should be used depends on the item to which they will be affixed. Some tags are designed to be placed on metal (such as computers or servers); some are designed for plastic and wood (but not metal); some are designed for hanging on an item; others have adhesives.

UHF tags do not interfere in any way with the HF tags that libraries put on their library materials because the frequencies over which each type of tag communicates are different (among other reasons). This also means the readers used for library material cannot also be used for UHF-tagged material.

The most commonly used readers for asset tracking are handhelds (a good example is the Motorola MC9090-Z), although fixed readers can also be used. While the readers cannot read both UHF and HF signals, they can read barcodes as well as UHF RFID tags, so it is easy to begin using RFID-based asset tags without having to cutover completely.

According to the 2012 RFID library survey, only 4 percent of US respondents are using RFID for asset tracking, which is similar to the United Kingdom (3 percent) but less than the Australian respondents (12 percent). Look for these numbers to increase dramatically by next year.[13]

Notes

1. See appendix D, "Encoding Data on the RFID Tag," in NISO RFID Revision Working Group, *RFID in U.S. Libraries*, Recommended Practice of the National Information Standards Organization, NISO RP-6-2012 (Baltimore, MD: NISO, March 2012), 52–67, www.niso.org/apps/group_public/download.php/8269/RP-6-2012_RFID-in_US_Libraries.pdf.
2. "3M Standard Interchange Protocol," version 2.00, document revision 2.12, updated April 11, 2006, http://multimedia.3m.com/mws/mediawebserver?mwsId=SSSSSu7zK1fslxtUm8_9m82Uev7qe17zHvTSevTSeSSSSSS--].
3. Mick Fortune, "SIP and the BIC Library Communications Framework," Book Industry Communication website, September 2011, www.bic.org.uk/e4libraries files/pdfs/110915%20blcf%20paper%20final.pdf.
4. For more information on NCIP, see "The NCIP Standard" on the NCIP NISO Standing Committee website, www.ncip.info/the-standard.html.
5. Mick Fortune, "The UK Data Standard—What Does It Mean?" *RFID—Changing Libraries for Good?* (blog). November 19, 2009, www.mickfortune.com/Wordpress/?p=176.
6. Fortune, "SIP and the BIC Library Communications Framework."
7. Book Industry Communication, "Library Interoperability Standards: Data Communication Framework for Library Systems," version 0.9, March 2011, www.bic.org.uk/e4librariesfiles/pdfs/110405%20Terminal%20applications%20v0.9.pdf.
8. Mick Fortune, e-mail communication with the author, March 18, 2012.
9. Jim Hopwood, "Beyond RFID Self Service," *CILIP Update*, February 2012. Available online to members only.
10. Ryan Livergood, "Buh Bye Library Card, Hello Smartphone (or, How NFC Might Replace Everything in

Your Wallet)," *Ryan Livergood* (blog), May 31, 2011, http://ryanlivergood.com/?p=173.

11. For a good explanation of NFC technology, see David Berkowitz, "RFID & NFC: How They Will Change Mobile . . . FOREVER!!!" presentation, March 14, 2011, www.slideshare.net/davidberkowitz/how-near-field-communications-nfc-and-radio-frequency-identification-rfid-will-change-mobile-sxsw-2011.

12. Dan Balaban, "The Year Ahead for NFC: Major M-Commerce Rollouts Unlikely until 2013," *NFC Times* (online magazine), December 23, 2011, www.nfctimes.com/report/year-ahead-nfc-major-m-commerce-rollouts-unlikely-until-2013.

13. Mick Fortune, "2012 Library RFID Survey: Stock Management," www.libraryrfid.co.uk/stockmanagement.html.

Library Technology Reports Respond to Your Library's Digital Dilemmas

Eight times per year, *Library Technology Reports* (*LTR*) provides library professionals with insightful elucidation, covering the technology and technological issues the library world grapples with on a daily basis in the information age.

Library Technology Reports 2012, Vol. 48	
January 48:1	**Bridging the Digital Divide with Mobile Services** by Andomeda Yelton
February/March 48:2	**Embedded Librarianship: Tools and Practices** by Buffy J. Hamilton
April 48:3	**Gadgets and Gizmos: Libraries and the Post–PC Era** by Jason Griffey
May/June 48:4	**Linked Data Tools: Connecting on the Web** by Karen Coyle
July 48:5	**RFID in Libraries: A Step toward Interoperability** by Lori Bowen Ayre
August/September 48:6	**Running the Digital Branch: Guidelines for Operating the Library Website** by David Lee King
October 48:7	**Making the Library More Accessible through Technology** by Char Booth
November/December 48:8	**Integrated Library Systems** by Marshall Breeding

ALA TechSource

alatechsource.org

ALA TechSource, a unit of the publishing department of the American Library Association

www.ingramcontent.com/pod-product-compliance
Lightning Source LLC
Chambersburg PA
CBHW080925300426

44115CB00018B/2949